T0271056

Empowering Women
in the Digital Economy

This book presents multidisciplinary perspectives on opportunities and best practices necessary for empowering women in the digital economy in developing countries. The book explores the components of connectivity that matter most to women. It also helps decision-makers and policymakers to adopt the policies needed to empower women in using digital platforms and developing (and taking up) careers in the digital economy in developing economies.

In response, we gathered eight contributions (or chapters) on new directions, strategies, and barriers to women's empowerment through digital technologies. The contributions span thematic areas such as female digital entrepreneurship, social media, and agricultural value chains, women in the gig economy, the digital divide, gender disparities in cryptocurrencies, and digital access in agriculture.

In précis, the contributions argue that, first, appropriate legislation matters, but it is not enough – there is a need to alter social and cultural attitudes and raise awareness. Second, there is a need to address affordability. Government and development agencies may begin by offering free or discounted smart devices to rural women and appropriate digital skills training relevant to their economic activities. Third, there is a need for urgent attention by government labor agencies in developing countries to enforce decent working conditions and protection for female gig workers whiles maximizing opportunities being offered through these platforms. **Don't just leave women to use digital platforms and services; support them with sound policies and programs for responsible and sustainable use.**

In effect, this book offers clarity on new strategies, case studies/examples, and lessons in addressing or circumventing institutional challenges to women's empowerment through digital technologies.

Empowering Women in the Digital Economy

A Quest for Meaningful Connectivity and Access in Developing Countries

Edited by

Sheena Lovia Boateng
University of Ghana, Accra, Ghana

Richard Boateng
University of Ghana, Accra, Ghana

Thomas Anning-Dorson
University of the Witwatersrand, South Africa

Routledge
Taylor & Francis Group

A PRODUCTIVITY PRESS BOOK

First published 2023
by Routledge
605 Third Avenue, New York, NY 10158

and by Routledge
4 Park Square, Milton Park, Abingdon, Oxon, OX14 4RN

Routledge is an imprint of the Taylor & Francis Group, an informa business

ISBN: 978-1-032-29850-4 (hbk)
ISBN: 978-1-032-29849-8 (pbk)
ISBN: 978-1-003-30234-6 (ebk)

DOI: 10.4324/9781003302346

Typeset in Garamond
by KnowledgeWorks Global Ltd.

This is dedicated to women creating a better world
for others and themselves through
digital technologies.

Contents

Foreword

Women's empowerment has become an opportune interest for policymakers, practitioners, entrepreneurs, and politicians worldwide. Hence, a contemporary text that explores how to create more winners than losers innovatively and responsibly in empowering women is a must-read. As this book rightly notes, the gender gap in the digital realm is undeniably a complicated and multifaceted issue. Hence, new perspectives on how to address the issue need to be shared globally and more frequently.

The new directions to women restructuring agricultural value chains through social media, digital access in agriculture, gender issues in the gig economy, female digital entrepreneurship, and gender disparities in the cryptocurrency economy are just the selection of the contributions, which provide new directions worth considering. The contributions also passionately advocate an urgency for government and other development agencies to address affordability and literacy barriers to digital devices, platforms, and services; create decent working conditions for gig work; and address vulnerabilities of female digital entrepreneurs. The response needed should be bold and responsible in a manner that enhances the meaningful connectivity, access, and use of digital technologies by women.

Written by management researchers and practitioners, I envisage this book will be an invaluable and indispensable reference to practitioners, researchers, policymakers, and students of gender studies, socio-economic development, marketing, human resource, information technology, and developing countries. I am hopeful the contributions will spur the necessary debates and discussions in the spaces that can generate a positive change to empower women in developing countries. Let this book inspire you to do more for women in developing countries.

Dr. Bryan Acheampong
Minister for Food and Agriculture, Republic of Ghana
Honorable Member of Parliament for Abetifi Constituency,
8th Parliament, Republic of Ghana

Preface

In developing economies, for example, women and girls are usually at a disadvantaged end in terms of participation in the digital economy as men often own and use computers and the Internet more than women and girls, spend more time online, enroll in more technology classes, demonstrate greater motivation to learn digital skills, and access and remain in digital jobs. In terms of access to job opportunities in the Information and Communications Technology (ICT) sector, for example, women tend to experience more challenges in their attempt to access and remain in digital jobs. This disadvantage may result from technological, social-cultural, and institutional barriers, especially for women in developing economies.

In this respect, the book presents multidisciplinary perspectives of opportunities and best practices necessary for empowering women in the digital economy in developing countries. The book engages this discourse from two perspectives – meaningful access and use of digital platforms and services and the uptake of careers in the digital economy. By meaningful connectivity and access, we refer to the instance of remaining digitally active online daily and policymakers on their part instituting measures and policies to ensure users are empowered whiles being digitally active. Thus, the book seeks to explore the components of connectivity that matter most to women and help decision-makers and policymakers to adopt the policies needed to empower women and girls in using digital platforms and developing (and taking up) careers in the digital economy in developing economies.

In response, we gathered eight contributions (or chapters) on new directions, strategies, and barriers to women's empowerment through digital technologies. The contributions span thematic areas such as female digital entrepreneurship, social media and agricultural value chains, women in the gig economy, the digital divide, gender disparities in cryptocurrencies, and digital access in agriculture.

In relation to the outcomes of meaningful connectivity and access, the first contribution explores the experiences of Filipino women entrepreneurs and their use of e-business as means for income-generating ventures during the Philippine economic-pandemic struggle. It suggests that e-business initiatives of Filipino women entrepreneurs tend to foster a culture of independence and financial freedom. It, therefore, proposes to champion Filipino women entrepreneurs' continuing transition into the digital economy. This framework offers directions applicable to other developing countries seeking to do the same.

The second contribution also highlights how women are taking up new careers – 'side businesses or side hustles' – by creating online retail businesses in the agricultural value chain using social media. The findings revealed that social media platforms address the operational challenges of time, location, cost, and process of running a business by female entrepreneurs in the agricultural value chain and can be meaningfully used to overcome some of the cultural barriers in empowering women in this sector. The findings also denote how these online retail initiatives are restructuring agricultural value chains as new entrants and thereby complementing their livelihood strategies.

The third contribution analyzes the effect of the digitalization of business operations on the empowerment of female entrepreneurs. The results show statistically significant positive effects of digitalization on the economic, relational, and personal and psychological empowerment of 158 female respondents. The study recommends that female entrepreneurs be oriented on understanding, using and effectively managing digital platforms and services to have positive returns on their investments and business operations. Concerning development agencies, including government and international agencies, there is a need to offer digital training programs and related assistance for female entrepreneurship development.

The fourth contribution examines the involvement of women in rural-based social institutions (BUMDes) in two tourist villages in Indonesia. It highlights the role of women in supporting the success of BUMDes in building the local tourism economy through social media and websites. These technology-enabled social institutions provide a broader space for women to develop their capacities. In addition to economic empowerment, BUMDes institutions provide a platform for social empowerment as women get to be actively involved in the social strata in the non-domestic realm. The study suggests that digitally enhancing women's participation in economic activities can accelerate development from the downstream.

The fifth contribution takes a step into the gig economy to examine the experiences of a female worker in the world of offering temporary and flexible labor services to consumers for a fee determined by an online platform. With a focus on the food delivery service, the findings show that women can earn relatively more from gig work than their earnings from 'some' regular jobs. There is evidence of economic empowerment as the case example is able to pay rent and support herself and her daughter through this gig work. However, familial responsibilities are often a constraint and adversely affect the number of hours worked and, as a result, earnings as a gig worker. On the other hand, there are largely no special concessions or considerations for women gig workers – such decisions are left to the discretion of platform dispatchers. There are also concerns of vulnerability to attacks and harassment, often with no recourse for help. The case study sheds a need for urgent attention by government labor agencies to enforce decent working conditions and protection for gig workers while maximizing opportunities being offered through these platforms.

The sixth contribution revisits the issue of the gender digital divide, with a specific emphasis on India, and examines how the findings can be used in creating and implementing practical solutions to bridge the gender digital gap in India and other developing countries. The findings highlight that women's access to and usage of digital technology and the Internet remains lower than men, even when women are educated, have sufficient income, and reside in urban areas. This disparity is more acute in rural areas. First, it is important to accept that the gender gap in the digital realm is undeniably a complicated and multifaceted issue. Legislation matters, but it is not enough – there is a need to alter social and cultural attitudes and raise awareness. Second, there is a need to address affordability. Government and development agencies may begin by offering free or discounted smart devices to rural women, coupled with appropriate digital skills training relevant to their economic activities.

The seventh contribution examines gender disparities in cryptocurrencies in developing and emerging economies. The chapter argues that while cryptocurrency, a major fin-tech product, is a potential instrument to accelerate financial inclusion, previous research on its usage among women remains very limited. Compared to women, men are more likely to own and trade cryptocurrencies and work in the blockchain and digital asset industries. In developing and emerging economies characterized by the lack of access to education and financial resources, as well as by cultural and societal biases, these disparities may get even more pronounced. Among other recommendations to address the gender gap in the cryptocurrency industry, it is important to increase women's education and awareness about cryptocurrency and to promote diversity and inclusion in the industry. It is also equally important to tell the story of women making strides in the industry and their related contextual solutions in order to address societal and cultural biases.

The eighth and final contribution explores digital access among new shea farming entrants. In northern Ghana, shea is a crucial resource for sustaining livelihoods and ensuring food security. The contribution of shea to the income and food security of collectors is reported to be about 21%, and this could be more for some livelihoods. New shea farming entrants refer to shea workers with five or fewer years of practice or experience in shea farming. Among the 540 respondents studied, there are more females (over 98%) as new entrants than males. From the device adoption perspective, about 88% own or have access to feature phones. Educated new shea farming entrants dominate those who own or have access to feature phones (89%). However, most of the new farmers do not own or have access to smartphones. Affordability remains the primary reason for the non-adoption, and digital skills literacy is a primary need for all new shea entrants. Improving access to affordable digital devices is a must. There is a need to train them to operate devices with minimal assistance and also to identify and use specific functions and applications, which are beneficial to their shea activities. For the uneducated, basic skills training in writing, reading, and numeracy are needed to enhance their capacity to leverage digital devices and services.

In précis, the contributions argue that, first, appropriate legislation matters, but it is not enough – there is a need to alter social and cultural attitudes and raise awareness. Second, there is a need to address affordability. Government and development agencies may begin by offering free or discounted smart devices to rural women, coupled with appropriate digital skills training relevant to their economic activities. Third, there is a need for urgent attention by government labor agencies in developing countries to enforce decent working conditions and protection for female gig workers while maximizing opportunities being offered through these platforms. Don't just leave women to use digital platforms and services; support them with sound policies and programs for responsible and sustainable use.

In effect, the eight chapters offer clarity on new strategies, case studies/ examples, and lessons in addressing or circumventing institutional challenges to women's empowerment through digital technologies.

We appreciate the contributions made to this book and the enormous time and effort put out to assist the double-blind review process. These contributors span more than ten universities, public- and private-sector institutions across the United Kingdom, India, Ghana, Indonesia, Philippines, and South Africa. We can confidently state that this book serves as an example of how academics and practitioners from Europe, Asia, and Africa may work effectively together for the benefit of women in developing countries. The fact that this book has provided a forum for such a nexus of knowledge is commendable, and we are happy about it.

Finally, and most importantly, we thank Kristine Rynne Mednansky, *Senior Editor, Taylor and Francis Group,* for continuously supporting us and managing the overall book project from the publisher's side.

We hope you will enjoy reading the book and applying the directions and perspectives communicated by these diverse contributions. We invite you to contact us for questions, feedback, and discussions.

Sheena Lovia Boateng, University of Ghana, Accra, Ghana

Richard Boateng, University of Ghana, Accra, Ghana

Thomas Anning-Dorson, University of the Witwatersrand, South Africa

Editorial Advisory Board

Joseph Budu, Ghana Institute of Management and Public Administration, Ghana

Owusu Acheampong, University of Ghana Business School, Ghana

Mansah Preko, University of Ghana Business School, Ghana

Endorsement

Women's empowerment has become an opportune interest for policymakers, practitioners, entrepreneurs, and politicians worldwide. Hence, a contemporary text that explores how to create more winners than losers innovatively and responsibly in empowering women is a must-read. As this book rightly notes, the gender gap in the digital realm is undeniably a complicated and multifaceted issue. Hence, new perspectives on how to address the issue need to be shared globally and more frequently. Let this book inspire you to do more for women in developing countries.

Dr. Bryan Acheampong
Minister for Food and Agriculture, Republic of Ghana
Honorable Member of Parliament for Abetifi Constituency,
8th Parliament, Republic of Ghana

Contributors

Lalit Anjana
University of Delhi, India

Thomas Anning-Dorson
University of the Witwatersrand,
    South Africa

Sabina Appiah-Boateng
University of Cape Coast,
    Ghana

Pasty Asamoah
Kwame Nkrumah University
    of Science and Technology,
    Ghana

Janet Serwah Boateng
University of Cape Coast,
    Ghana

Richard Boateng
University of Ghana Business
    School, Ghana

Sheena Lovia Boateng
University of Ghana Business
    School, Ghana

Joseph Budu
Ghana Institute of Management
    and Public Administration,
    Ghana

Ana Leah Dungog-Cuizon
University of the Philippines,
    Philippines

Edward Entee
University of Ghana Business
    School, Ghana

Catherine V. Hernando
University of the Philippines,
    Philippines

Isaac Kosi
University of Cape Coast, Ghana

Mavis Serwah Benneh Mensah
University of Cape Coast,
    Ghana

M. Zaenul Muttaqin
Cenderawasih University,
    Indonesia

Jan Brithney L. Navales
University of the Philippines,
  Philippines

Mymar Denise B. Nellas
University of the Philippines,
  Philippines

Martin Boakye Osei
Bournemouth University, United
  Kingdom

Obed Kwame Adzaku Penu
University of Ghana Business
  School, Ghana

Rohim Rohim
STIA Pembangunan, Indonesia

Rizza J. Sanchez
University of the Philippines,
  Philippines

Richelle S. Seares
University of the Philippines,
  Philippines

John Serbe Marfo
Kwame Nkrumah University
  of Science and Technology,
  Ghana

Made Selly Dwi Suryanti
Cenderawasih University,
  Indonesia

Chapter 1

E-Women in E-Business: Philippine Digital Entrepreneurship Initiatives during the Economic-Pandemic Struggle

Catherine V. Hernando, Mymar Denise B. Nellas,
Richelle S. Seares, Jan Brithney L. Navales,
Rizza J. Sanchez, and Ana Leah Dungog-Cuizon
*Cebu College of Social Sciences, University of the Philippines,
Gorordo Ave., Lahug, Cebu City, Philippines*

Contents

DOI: 10.4324/9781003302346-1

Introduction

A Filipina's place in the economy is mainly constrained to the informal economy, care work both domestic and international, and for the majority, in micro, small, and medium enterprises (MSMEs). In the Philippines, women-owned businesses are traditionally known to lag behind businesses led by their male counterparts in terms of size, productivity, and profitability. Women's entrepreneurship often operates in society's most disadvantaged sectors and even the lower ends of the value chain. There are certain limitations to their activities, granting them few opportunities for valuable business and growth.

The economic limitations imposed on women in the country have only worsened at the onset of the COVID-19 pandemic. The state has opted to lead an economic response through the Department of Trade and Industry (DTI)'s financing arm, the Small Business Corporation with the Bayanihan COVID-19 Assistance to Restart Enterprises (CARES) program, which is mandated to provide MSMEs with urgent relief needed to restart their businesses amid the pandemic. As of February 2021, 21,695 loans had been filed and approved (Balikbayan Media Center, 2021), a minuscule percentage of the total population of aspiring entrepreneurs hoping to at least tide the pandemic over.

With the COVID-19 pandemic limiting physical associations, obstacles to the economic sector are exacerbated, especially when severe restrictions are imposed upon traditional brick-and-mortar businesses, forcing a bulk of them to search for new mediums for selling their products and with the already available online platforms. This is the same for start-up entrepreneurs who are forced to enter new finance-generating activities to make up for job loss, both personal and of the spouse in the household. Given the ubiquity of the Internet and its indiscriminate access channels, both transitioning and start-up businesses are placed on equal footing, at least in terms of access to online avenues for business.

E-business has been undergoing a rise due to the availability of the Internet and online channels. Commonly utilized social media platforms are Facebook, Twitter, and Instagram, where potential customers are abundant. Additional advantages and incentives further motivate new entrepreneurs to choose online mediums to facilitate their businesses, including but not limited to (Yandug et al., 2020):

1. Online channels give free-market platforms.
2. Has a wide audience and customer reach.
3. Allows the establishment of customer relationships.
4. Provide free advertising posting and reach.

Filipino women have creatively resorted to various initiatives to engage in business via e-commerce platforms to combat the struggle of the economic pandemic. They have taken advantage of these platforms, which serve as an avenue for a wide variety of businesses where consumers are becoming more adaptable to online goods (McNulty, 2020). Filipino enterprises have embraced the use of e-commerce sites as a new marketing strategy. They are observed to have potential growth, especially since the COVID-19 outbreak has accelerated industry growth by transferring major retailers to an Internet platform for market sustainability (Ken Research, 2021).

DTI has established itself as the forerunner body in launching programs and roadmaps to improve the situation in the online business environment for the benefit and safety of all its stakeholders. In its recent launch of the E-Commerce 2022 Roadmap, the department has stated its situation, goals, and, more importantly, challenges that need to be conquered (DTI eCommerce, 2021). However, its vision has not narrowed down on the specific struggles and needs of women and has not considered the significant effects of the COVID-19 pandemic, which are two variables that this chapter aims to consider. The discussion investigates how the state responds to women's economic struggle and how Filipino women entrepreneurs use the Internet for ICT-based business as a solution for income-generating means and sales during the COVID-19 economic struggle. Specifically, it seeks to enumerate the finance-gathering initiatives taken up by women to address the economic pandemic struggle and how the rise of Filipina digital entrepreneurs during the COVID-19 pandemic was affected by cultural, economic, and psycho-social expectations that impacted their state of mind and business opportunities

The analysis discussed in this chapter will be the basis for a recommendation on government institutions' programs, activities, and projects (PAPs), concerning women's financial assistance considering the COVID-19 pandemic. To ensure stabilization and recovery post-COVID-19, women's access to critical support services should be guaranteed. Actions that provide business continuity and the means to re-activate business activity and build long-term resilience are essential.

Methodology

This section of the chapter explains the various methodologies to be used to conduct the study. The research methodology employed is a qualitative, descriptive case study that integrates a purposive sampling method for data analysis. The present study's research design incorporates purposive sampling. In qualitative research, sampling strategies often represent diverse perspectives and experiences rather than replicate their frequency on the broader population (Ziebland & McPherson, 2006). The researchers examined the phenomenon of women being involved in online businesses and using the Internet as a digital platform for income-generating during the pandemic.

This study will make use of researcher-made interview questions to provide a suitable data collection. The research instrument was validated by a few experts from the academe, business, and government sectors before it was laid on to the study (see Appendix B for the researcher-made questionnaires). The researchers utilized these platforms in gathering the data: Government Websites, Google Docs, Facebook, Facebook Messenger, and Google Meet. To prepare and guide the respondents before the actual interview virtually via Google Meet, the researchers sent a file highlighting critical information and queries through Google Docs. This step is also necessary to present the informed consent and preliminary data needed to be accomplished and filled out before administering the gathering of data from the respondents. After this, a Google Meet link was sent to the participants to conduct the interview properly once the necessary information was accomplished. The researchers transcribed and recorded all the interviews with the permission of the respondents.

Finally, the study will incorporate Colaizzi's method as a mode of analysis to give meaning to the genuine experiences of the new women entrepreneurs at the onset of the COVID-19 pandemic. This method of analysis will involve seven steps (Praveena & Sasikumar, 2021). First, participants' experiences as recorded in the transcript will be read and reread by the researchers to obtain a general understanding of their experiences. Next, significant statements will be extracted from the transcript. This will be followed by the formulation of meanings derived from the compiled significant statements. Meanings will then be organized into themes and clusters, after which there will be an integration and detailed description. After this, it is expected that the fundamental structure of the phenomenon studied can be formulated. Finally, a thorough discussion and analysis of the gathered data will be supplemented to establish a legitimized interpretation of the participants' experiences as E-women. Hence, the overall approach of this study relatively focuses on the government institutions' programs to combat economic challenges and Filipina's sociocultural and economic outlook during the pandemic.

Identification of Research Locale and Respondents

The Region VII of the Philippines, Central Visayas, consists of four provinces: Cebu, Bohol, Negros Oriental, and Siquijor, one of the most developed regional economies and the fourth largest regional economy in the country, equipped with various industries ranging from footwear, furniture, food processing, and ICT-based services and electronics, was identified as the research locale (Department of Trade and Industry, 2018).

To achieve the research objectives, six (6) women online entrepreneurs from the top (3) urbanized provinces of Cebu, Bohol, and Negros Oriental were selected as respondents. The first three respondents received state-led assistance from the government through DTI's Bayanihan CARES Program, while the remaining three relied on individual-finance gathering initiatives as sources of capital.

The first respondent, *R1FB*, is from the Province of Bohol and juggles three jobs before and during the pandemic: a manager of a local distribution company, a real estate agent, and a food seller, who then operated in the physical set-up but shifted to the online platform. The second respondent, *R2CN*, is from the Province of Cebu, works at a company's Human Resource Unit, and is a city distributor of skincare products. The third respondent, *R3JB*, is from the Province of Bohol, served as a local public servant, and is now baking pastries full-time and selling them through physical and online platforms. The fourth respondent, *R4MS*, is from the Province of Cebu, taught as a tertiary teacher and offered tutorial services before the pandemic, and currently owns an online clothing shop. The fifth respondent, *R5HR*, is from the Province of Cebu; she maintained a four-year job in the banking industry before quitting and starting her online businesses in footwear and skincare. The last and sixth respondent, *R6BA*, is from the Province of Negros Oriental and depended on allowances and academic-related commissions as a college student before teaming up with her sister in an online crochet business.

Exclusion and Inclusion Criteria

The case study only included businesses owned by Filipino women entrepreneurs from Region VII that started or shifted and restarted (in the case of the state-led beneficiaries) from March 2020 until the present and are currently active and operating in digital online platforms.

Discussion and Analysis

To analyze the data obtained from the respondents, online women entrepreneurs from Central Visayas, the researchers classified the emergent themes into four categories: pandemic effect on entrepreneurs, finance-gathering initiatives of Filipina women entrepreneurs, gendered experiences of E-women entrepreneurs, and challenges of digitized set-up. Tables 1.1–1.4 indicate the formulated meaning, theme clusters, and emergent themes. The formulated meaning was drawn from the direct significant statements of the respondents during the online interview. At the same time, the theme clusters were the common categories of these meanings that were further categorized into emergent themes.

Effects of the Pandemic on Women Entrepreneurs

The coronavirus disease (COVID-19), aside from causing health sector setbacks, resulted in a massive economic shock (Bartik et al., 2020).

Table 1.1   Effects of the Pandemic on Women Entrepreneurs

Formulated Meanings	Theme Clusters	Emergent Theme
The respondent works as HR in the company and has an online business for extra income The respondent works as a teacher and tutors students as a side job.	The businesswomen had steady paying jobs before the pandemic. While working, they also have side-hustles for extra income.	A necessity of multiple sources of income
The respondent stopped her business for two months during the pandemic. The respondent observes that during this ongoing pandemic, a lot of businesses have closed. Personally, she continues her business in little ways.	The entrepreneurs have suffered losses in income. Businesses closed during the pandemic.	Pandemic restrictions have a bad effect on business

However, the burden on women is greater because reproductive and productive works are converging in one setting – the home.

The emergent themes for Table 1.1 are as follows: the necessity of multiple sources of income and pandemic restrictions negatively affect business.

The Necessity of Multiple Sources of Income

By necessity of multiple sources of income, the researchers mean that a woman has to wear many hats and take on more than one job to sustain herself and her family financially. This was the case of the respondent, R2CN, when she revealed:

> My number one source of income is my job as an employee of a certain company. Also, I am into selling anything on the side.

During the interview, R2CN started the discussion by highlighting her current situation as a single mother of her 12-year-old daughter. Although they received an allotment from her father, she still has to meet ends for her child's education.

Pandemic Restrictions Have a Bad Effect on Business

The pandemic health protocol and restrictions were detrimental to physical business operations. This was the case of respondent R1FB when she expressed:

> Aside from the African Swine Flu Fever, COVID-19 brought so many restrictions. Until now, our physical store is closed and we continued it online.

R1FB further added that because of this, her business stopped from April to June 2020. She recalled that the business' previous profit went to the store's renovation, the fixed asset, making fast recovery impossible. She resorted to purely online food selling after two to three months of inactivity to save her business. Until now, she stated that she is still anxious to open a physical store since a lockdown might occur again.

Cherie Blair Foundation for Women (2021) reported similar findings that 83.3% of the women surveyed concluded that the pandemic had negatively influenced their businesses, and 38.5% of them would or may decide to close it. Moreover, Mustafa et al. (2021) also liquidated in their findings that there is a necessity for women-led businesses to undertake creativity and digitalization to survive during the pandemic.

Considering the emergent themes from the data gathered, it can be concluded that a woman entrepreneur, despite the household and market challenges thrown by the pandemic, managed to juggle multiple sources of income to sustain life's basic needs, business expenses, and the pandemic's added costs. Subsequently, they took the digital platform by storm to rescue their businesses from bankruptcy utilizing various marketing strategies.

Finance-Gathering Initiatives of Filipina Entrepreneurs

Women perform varied finance-gathering initiatives. Some are individual-led, pertaining to those Filipino women entrepreneurs who independently strive to generate funds to establish their online business. Meanwhile, there are also Filipino women entrepreneurs who were backed up by the state through government institutions, specifically the DTI, which extended assistance to Filipino entrepreneurs through Small Business Corporation's "*Bayanihan* CARES Program."

Though Ahmad (2012) noted that advantages and incentives inspire budding entrepreneurs to use the Internet as a platform to help them run their businesses. The same result is shown in Table 1.2 – Finance-gathering

Table 1.2   Finance Gathering Initiatives of Filipina Entrepreneurs (Part 1)

Formulated Meaning	Theme Clusters	Emergent Theme
The respondent funds her business using personal savings and salary from her job The respondent recommends this program to other Filipina entrepreneurs especially because it has no interest and has a grace period before the start of payment. The respondent believes that the loan she received was not enough but at least it was able to help a little.	Funded their online business with personal savings and with the help of family members. Took a small loan from government programs with zero interest and a long grace period before payment starts. The loan from the state was small but at least it helped a little in their business.	Varied sources of capital for online business
The respondent recalls her experience as a Facebook e-business seller from when she was younger selling fan merchandise The respondent is a teacher who worries about her salary in a time where schools are closed down. She decides to pursue e-business as she has a family to sustain their needs. The respondent expresses how the business helped her staff. The respondent shares that online business does not need to use traditional methods in selling since technology is within the palm of your hands. The respondent highlights the safety that the online business offers to women entrepreneurs.	Exposed to business even in their younger years. The income from the e-business becomes an addition to their current savings and supports them and their families. Giving importance to employees who helped sustain the business amid pandemic. The advantages of social media boost the credibility of their online business thus appealing to more customers the opportunity to earn within the comfort of their homes with lesser expenses. Securing safety from the dangers of having physical stores and the privacy a woman wanted to secure as a business owner.	Crucial reasons for entering online business Advantages of engaging in online business

initiatives of Filipina entrepreneurs taking technology as a new method to engage in e-commerce.

Varied Sources of Capital for Online Business

The first emerging theme presented above under this aspect is the *Varied Sources of Capital for Online Business*. This was subdivided into two specific sources, personal savings and government loans, wherein personal savings refer to the amount of money that has been set aside for non-immediate use. In contrast, government loans pertain to financing programs initiated by the state to assist MSMEs in restarting businesses due to the economic downturn caused by the pandemic. In this regard, R1FB revealed,

> Before the pandemic, I have my own personal savings from my salary, commissions, and incentives as a real estate agent.

Studies have shown that about 60% of successful start-up businesses are funded with personal savings (Pena, 2002). It is common for many entrepreneurs to rely on the available resources they have to capitalize on new business opportunities.

Part of entrepreneurial growth is to find alternatives that could expand businesses. Filipino women entrepreneurs have opted to finance additional capital from state subsidies to bring back losses obtained by the economic drop caused by the pandemic. Thus, some respondents have decided to opt for government loans to restart their businesses, particularly the DTI's COVID-19 Assistance to Restart Enterprises (CARES) program. R2CN expresses this acquisition of state-led initiatives,

> I applied for an online loan from DTI under SBCorp.

The statements provided conclusions that women in the economic industry find ways to sustain their businesses despite the risks and downturns in trying to revive the economy. However, inevitable repercussions need to be improved with this state-led subsidy for entrepreneurs. As R2CN disclosed,

> From my experience, one thing I didn't appreciate was the waiting time..., and then actually the loan was inadequate for the online business that I have right now). Respondent R3JB revealed that, ...

It is really not enough but I am still thankful for the initial help they (government) have given.

This correspondingly turns out that even with the flexible terms and conditions under the Small Business Corporation, the loan provided by the state is small, but it indeed did a little help in their businesses.

Crucial Reasons for Entering Online Business

The second emerging theme shown in Table 1.2 corresponds to the crucial reasons for entering online business. First, it is observed that these women entrepreneurs acquire beforehand initial knowledge of business management, which urged them to start a business. Research suggests that entrepreneurs are more likely to come from homes where a parent initially owns a business (Cooper & Dunkelberg, 1987). Additionally, women's decision to set up their venture is also influenced by resources that may be available and circumstances (Yukongdi & Cañete, 2020). R4MS, who came from a family of entrepreneurs, expounded,

In my case, this is the background I grew up to. My parents are both in the field of business, so I was preconditioned ever since that I will start my own business.

Pihie and Bagheri (2010) stated that family influence is an essential factor that provides the background experience and motivation to start entrepreneurial activities.

Second, another crucial factor why Filipino women started an online business is that it opens up an avenue for an extra source of income or even becomes the primary source of income. Furthermore, this allows the entrepreneurial spirit of women to venture into different opportunities in business. As R5HR shared,

I was thinking why not try to go venture in entrepreneurship? Who would know, if I'll be successful in this? So, I risk without knowing if I'll be successful.

Managing uncertainty in a global pandemic is a risk that incorporates coping strategies to ensure the outcome of an organized business. These women-owned businesses have been through tantamount losses, adding up their initial capital to sustain their businesses.

The third critical point is the maternal and familial instincts women have. Most of the women frequently reported in previous studies testified the need to provide for and supplement the needs of their families (Yukongdi & Cañete, 2020). A case in point is the experience of R2MS, who is a wife and a mother of a toddler, who started an online clothing business at the onset of the COVID-19 pandemic,

> My husband is the main motivator why I started my online business at the same time is my baby. R2CN, a single mother who juggles multiple businesses, valued the same sentiments with R2MS, Actually, the main reason is to have an extra income, for my twelve-year-old daughter.

According to them, being a mother and an entrepreneur was not an easy job. As Dattani (2020) found similar findings, women business owners are dealing with intensified social reproduction duties, household labor imbalances, and the need for extra income-generating activities caused by the pandemic.

An altruistic reason obtained in this study is the ability to support employees or the workforce in dire need of jobs during a pandemic. These women entrepreneurs generously thought of the well-being of their employees. As R1FB narrated,

> My business can help my staff. This is how I look at my business and how it would be able to support my employees. A family can eat because of this business. Currently, I have nine (9) staff, so I am able to feed nine families ...

R1FB further added that without the people working for her, the online business she stood for would never be a success without them. Thus, she feels indebted to continue despite the ongoing pandemic for the sake of her employees.

Advantages of Engaging in Online Business

The third emerging theme stipulated in Table 1.2 is the presented advantages of engaging in online business for women entrepreneurs. It is crucial to consider how these women manage to gather income having the benefits of e-commerce. According to McNulty (2020), online platforms serve as an avenue that supports many businesses where consumers are becoming more adaptable to online goods. R1FB enumerated the advantages when she started her online business,

> The advantage for online business is that it caters a wide reach for clients. Traditional marketing methods like tarpaulins, newspapers, radio, or flyers are not anymore needed. But this time, the target is already budget boosting (for Facebook posts) for your target audience. Basic transactions are easier since I can monitor them through our controller. And even our operations, we just have Messenger as our medium.

It is beneficial for R1FB and even for other women online entrepreneurs the broad scope of online platforms to sell products through e-commerce. Moreover, social media boosts the credibility of their online business, thus appealing to more customers with an opportunity to earn within the comfort of their homes with lesser expenses.

Aside from the fact that the online platform has made everything accessible from wide coverage, availability of courier services, cashless payments, and remote operations, another important factor for the respondent is their safety. There are risks to security and safety when managing physical store set-up. An example shared by R2CN explains how she finds it better for women entrepreneurs to manage an online business since being in a physical store set-up intends precautions from robbery and burglary that may take place anytime.

This implies that women need to double their security when operating on-site businesses. Thus, as found in this study, females see social media as a safe platform to conduct their business operations. Hence, to concur with Alampay (2008), individual Filipino entrepreneurs and small businesses venture into e-commerce by utilizing the Internet through social networking websites and mobile phone-based cash systems because of its reliable, secure, and accessible means.

Marketing Strategies for the Online Business

Another emerging theme shown in Table 1.3 refers to the marketing strategies for online business that the Filipina entrepreneurs acquired while establishing an online business. These pertain to a combination of online and technical skills learned such as cooking, graphic design, captioning and

Table 1.3 Finance Gathering Initiatives of Filipina Entrepreneurs (Part 2)

Formulated Meanings	Theme Clusters	Emergent Themes
The respondent learns of skills in cooking and recently the online skills to create e-posters of her own through Canva, which has allowed her to save up on promotion because she does the work herself.	New skills are learned from the experience of managing an e-business and help is enlisted from friends, family, and colleagues from starting up a business to maintaining it.	Marketing strategies for online business
The respondent believes that no man is an island and enlists help from friends and family for boosting her content. For editing, she does it alone and makes use of YouTube video tutorials and Google as a reference.	State-led programs are sought out to help women build their business and sustain it during the economic pandemic struggle.	
The respondent enlists the help of her graduating nephews and nieces who have more free time in this modular setup to help in managing her e-business, particularly in computer literacy.	Entrepreneurs come up with innovative and creative ideas to usher audiences to get into their products and boost their sales. They do research and make use of the vast amount of knowledge and reference that YouTube and Google provide.	
The respondent points out that skills in captioning and correspondence with customers are necessary in e-business because they are what help an e-business survive.		
The respondent taps people who can help her because managing an e-business is an arduous task. It's not just about posting and immediately getting clients; there is a need to be innovative because online competition is very tight.	The e-business becomes a collaborative effort between the entrepreneur and the people around her who offer help in managing the business like her family, friends, friends of friends, colleagues, and even acquaintances. There is the mutual responsibility of ensuring an income for the entrepreneur and her employees.	
The respondent develops skills in PR or product reviews by influencers to boost sales for her business. She gives a PR every month and sees a growth in sales all over the Philippines. For her, the online platform is an avenue to grow both your audience and sales at the same time.		
The respondent shares her word-of-mouth marketing strategy is useful if one has the confidence that the product you are selling is indeed effective.	Generating creative marketing strategies of products through online platforms especially Facebook increases sales and income of online businesses.	
The respondent notes how friends, friends of friends, and family boost her business through shares, thereby increasing sales and improving branding.		

editing, computer and social media literacy, accounting, product review, and promotion of products. This is the case in point of the experience of R1FB who claimed that:

> Just recently, I learned an online skill on how to create e-posters of my own through Canva … just last year.

With the new online skills acquired, i.e., editing and graphic design using Canva, R1FB created her e-posters and reduced costs since this allowed her to save up on promotion because she does the work herself. The e-business also became a collaborative effort between the entrepreneur and her family, friends, acquaintances, and even customers. This is true in the case of R1FB who said:

> I think it really helped. I receive support which can help increase and boost my sales because whenever I post online, most of my family and friends share it, and then the friends of my friends will share it too, and so on. That is why my sales and branding increased. So, it really takes a community to build a business.

Moreover, by learning more skills to market products online with e-commerce and the usage of social media platforms to gain more followers and customers, we mean that the shared experiences of the respondents reveal that these businesswomen generated creative marketing strategies in online platforms such as Facebook intending to boost sales, audience reach, and income. These entrepreneurs hold the view that online competition is very tight, and thus, this challenges them to have more innovative ideas. This is true in the case of R5HR, who revealed that:

> Influencer marketing through product reviews is a big help for me. My sales increased as well as my audience reach. For example, in my footwear online business, I usually give products monthly to the influencers whom I know for product reviews. I can really see its positive effect on the growth of my sales and audience in Manila and even other parts of the Philippines. So, that is one way that I know which is good for online business.

Because female entrepreneurs have resorted to starting or restarting businesses and flexibly adapt by learning new online skills and generating creative marketing strategies by taking advantage of the available online platforms and e-commerce sites, the conclusion is that their respective online businesses have been able to thrive during the economic pandemic struggle. It enabled them to acquire both online and technical skills and boost or increase their sales and customer reach, thereby maintaining their income and sustaining their livelihood. This is also what is mentioned in literature on online businesses, which reveals that Filipino enterprises have embraced the use of e-commerce sites as a new marketing strategy and are observed to have potential growth, especially since the COVID-19 outbreak has accelerated industry growth by transferring major retailers to an Internet platform for market sustainability (Ken Research, 2021). Thus, this trend necessitates upskilling and reskilling Filipino women entrepreneurs through online training and programs about digital entrepreneurship and e-commerce marketing.

Long-Term Plans for E-Business

The last emerging theme shown in Table 1.4 matches the Filipina entrepreneurs' long-term plans for their e-business. This refers to the respondents' plans to expand their reach through franchising and

Table 1.4   Finance Gathering Initiatives of Filipina Entrepreneurs (Part 3)

Formulated Meanings	Theme Clusters	Emergent Themes
The respondent plans for her expanding business (Papa G's) through franchising while using the online platform for promotions. The respondent aims to establish a physical store at the same time, to continue the online business since it contributes a lot in marketing and expanding the target audience. The respondent sees the good of continuing the online business. She deems that the online platforms saved her business. Thus, she decides not to stop.	Establishing a physical store while utilizing the online platform for marketing strategies. Continuing the online business since it positively contributed financially and mentally to the businesses and the owners respectively.	Long-term plans for e-business

continuing the business operation by establishing a physical store while capitalizing on online marketing strategies. As R1FB said:

> So, my plan for Papa G is for expansion. And usually, we can see how the promotion of franchising works now online. So again, it goes back to online by using Facebook.

Also, this emerging theme means that the online business has become a supplementary yet significant factor to the physical business since these online platforms functioned mainly as marketing and advertising tools. This is true in the case of R5HR who shared:

> I really like to have my own physical store, that's my goal. I have a physical store and at the same time, I'll continue operating online because, for me, online business is a big help, especially in marketing and targeting your audience.

Gendered Experiences of E-Women Entrepreneurs

Women entrepreneurs have been forced to adapt to the economic challenges exacerbated by COVID-19. In the past two years, women have had to be innovative and flexible to grab economic opportunities. The experience of E-women in the pandemic is reflective of both their struggle and their success.

The emergent themes for Table 1.5 are as follows: perceptions of women in business, the economic impact of the availability of business opportunities to women, and the psycho-social impact of Filipina's state of mind on financial support and independence.

Perceptions of Women in Business

The researchers found that there was no perceived discrimination based on gender. Social, cultural, and marital expectations were seen only as an effect of cohabitation for some, while others received support and encouragement. Per the case of R1FB, social and cultural expectations do not limit a woman in business. In fact, it is seen as an advantage.

She said: "I have never experienced those kinds of challenges because I am a woman. In fact, I think it is an advantage."

Table 1.5   Gendered Experiences of E-Women Entrepreneurs (Part 1)

Formulated Meanings	Theme Clusters	Emergent Themes
The respondent does not encounter social and cultural expectations of being a businesswoman and perceives it as an advantage. The respondent experiences limitations of being a woman like physical endurance and patience. The respondent believes the strength and skill of women in marketing especially through word of mouth and emphasizes its advantage compared to men's limitations like being timid. The respondent knows the prevalence of gender equality in the economic sphere in society.	Instead of perceiving it as a challenge, the businesswomen claim that being a female entrepreneur is more of an advantage because of their skills in marketing and networking as well as soft skills like diligence and perseverance in achieving a successful business. Some entrepreneurs experience the physical limitations of being a woman. Businesswomen observe gender equality in terms of economic opportunities for women in society. In achieving success in their business, some businesswomen face social, cultural, and marital expectations as an effect of cohabitation while others receive support and encouragement.	Perceptions of women in business

To support this R2CN's case also emphasized the power of the female. To her, gender equality is present in the sphere of Philippine economic society. She said: "For me, women hold a more powerful position in the world of business because of their marketing skills like word of mouth. Women are very good at that compared to men who are often timid, at least those that I've encountered."

To add, R3JB and R4MS, both of whom were married women, admitted that expectations for Filipina entrepreneurs rose particularly during cohabitation, especially when extended families were involved and in need of support (Table 1.6).

Respondent R5HR encapsulates Filipina entrepreneurs by saying: "Nowadays, I see that a lot more women want to be successful."

Table 1.6   Gendered Experiences of E-Women Entrepreneurs (Part 2)

Formulated Meanings	Theme Clusters	Emergent Theme
The respondent notices her increase of income this time as she started her online business during this pandemic period. The respondent observes that her budgeted salary before she started online selling is simple and fixed, but now she acknowledges more income through her side hustles. She observes the greater economic opportunities available for women and the importance of grabbing those opportunities. The respondent observes more female entrepreneurs than male entrepreneurs in online business as well as the expansion of economic opportunities for women. The respondent sees and experiences the greater opportunities in online business. The respondent understands the factors to be considered when engaging in online business especially acquiring new skills.	Gender equality and women's economic opportunities in business are pervasive and are the common perspective among female entrepreneurs. Admitting a fixed salary is merely budgeted on a monthly basis. Being in e-business gained financial freedom and independence when it comes to finances and budget.	Economic impact of the availability of business opportunities to women.

Economic Impact of the Availability of Business Opportunities to Women

According to the article "Necessity or Opportunity? The Effects of State Fragility and Economic Development on Entrepreneurial Efforts," José Ernesto Amorós et al. espoused that the opportunity-based individual entrepreneurial (OPP) efforts are affected by the fragility of the state and the current state of the economy. Per the Institutional Theory of Entrepreneurship, the fragility of the state is indirectly proportional to opportunity-based individual entrepreneurial efforts (OPPs) and directly proportional to necessity-based entrepreneurial (NEC) endeavors. Meaning, the fragility of the state has a positive effect on NEC endeavors in contrast to

OPP efforts. The researchers found that the Philippines has displayed state fragility throughout the COVID-19 timeline, meaning, it has been inadequate in protecting citizens who lack or have lost formal employment throughout the pandemic. Hence, women have opted to initiate NEC endeavors and have created business opportunities for themselves through revolutionary alternate business methods of e-business.

Women entrepreneurs hold the greater appeal in marketing products due to their natural and technical skills in marketing, making them flexible in business engagement. This is expressed in R6BA's case.

R6BA stressed: "You know better because you are a woman. You have the advantage in selling products for women."

These cases solidify that women have greater economic opportunities due to gender equality in the business industry. Filipina entrepreneurs were also found to have gained financial freedom and independence through both corporate jobs and engaging in e-business.

Per the case of R2CN, her pre-pandemic income was stable. She initially had sidelines too, but she noticed an increase in income after founding her own online business. She said: "The main difference was that pre-pandemic I had already had side jobs, but they weren't much. During the pandemic, I started my online business, and from there, I was able to say I had earned a lot more which I've added to my budget."

The Internet has made it possible to earn online, and Filipino women entrepreneurs have grabbed this opportunity to revolutionize earnings during the economic pandemic struggle. It is one of the best modes of employment (Kuek et al., 2015).

R5HR and R6BA expressed that amid COVID-19, greater economic opportunities in the form of online platforms emerged for women, and it was necessary to grab those opportunities (Table 1.7).

Specifically, R6BA stressed that: "With e-business, I realized that women could engage in business. I realized that women can also actually earn money through this platform, thereby widening economic opportunities for women."

Psycho-Social Impact of Filipina's State of Mind on Financial Support and Independence

Online business shapes the female entrepreneurs' outlook and plays a major factor in achieving financial freedom, independence, and peace of mind.

In the case of R1FB, she expressed that online business is a revolutionary means of employment that brings along all new opportunities for women

Table 1.7   Gendered Experiences of E-Women Entrepreneurs (Part 3)

Formulated Meanings	*Theme Clusters*	*Emergent Theme*
The respondent believes in attaining freedom when a person is financially independent and considers online business as the greatest factor that shapes her outlook. The respondent considers online business as a big factor that shapes her outlook on financial independence. The respondent highlights the benefits and achievements of being financially independent like having authentic freedom in life and peace of mind.	Having an online business along with the opportunities it brings is a major factor that can shape the businesswomen's outlook on acquiring new skills, financial independence, authentic freedom, peace of mind, and a sense of pride for the female entrepreneurs.	Psycho-social impact of Filipina's state of mind on financial support and independence.

entrepreneurs. In the process, women learn new skills and integrate their already existing skills into online business management. She expressed feeling a sense of freedom and peace of mind being able to earn at home: "Online business offers a big opportunity. I only work at my desk but I earn a lot for my source of income."

She further added that she gained financial freedom in terms of buying what she wants and also the decisions she makes in life: "It's really a big factor once you are financially independent. You don't wait for someone to give you money, you can do whatever you want. It's limitless. That is the biggest factor."

Women entrepreneurs feel a sense of pride after founding their online businesses and working for their success. R5HR stressed that: "My online business helped me stand on my own. At the same time, I can do whatever I want. In terms of money-making, although I don't have a background in marketing or business, I was still able to establish a brand and a small business at the same time thanks to these online means. I am proud to have established my own business."

Table 1.8   Challenges in the Digitized Set-Up (Part 1)

Formulated Meanings	Theme Clusters	Emergent Themes
The respondent shares that for suspicious accounts, she verifies their FB account. The respondent gladly answers that she did not encounter any bogus buyers or scammers.	Accepting orders or transactions from people you personally know or from legit referrals to intercept bogus buyers.	Fear of fraudulent transactions. Need for accredited buyers, suppliers, and clients to avoid scam.

Challenges in the Digitized Set-Up

In this section, the challenges faced by women entrepreneurs are enumerated and analyzed. The focus is narrowed down on their experienced challenges in the current digitized setup precisely: in facilitating their business online and their online transactions with the government, as affected by the pandemic restrictions and guidelines (Table 1.8).

Issues in Online Business

On the business side of things, DTI eCommerce (2021) identifies the rise of fraudulent transactions that shows the country's weak consumer protection regulations as one of the challenges in the e-commerce industry. Fortunately, this has not been the case for any of the interviewed women in this study. In R3JB's words,

> In my case, ma'am, so far, I have not encountered this kind [scam transactions] of problem.

But while they have not experienced this personally, stories of other online entrepreneurs victimized by fraudulent purchases actively circulate on the Internet, thus urging them to take extra measures to prevent this problem. The shared practice by all the interviewed women is to verify the authenticity of each online purchase by checking the buyer's account for authenticity, as evident in the case of R1FB (Table 1.9).

Internet Dependence and Technical Skills

However, despite the respondent's respite on this issue, two overarching problems, specifically (1) Internet Connectivity-Dependence of women

Table 1.9 Challenges in the Digitized Set-Up (Part 2)

Formulated Meanings	Theme Clusters	Emergent Theme
The respondent shared that in the online transaction required by the loan, she had to enlist help from her child who is an IT student. She shares that she is computer-illiterate. The respondent shares that nowadays she is very dependent on the Internet. Without the Internet, she will not be able to operate her business. The respondent shares that she feels a little hassle in the online transaction with the government. She has to upload, scan, and photograph. The respondent shares that in the KMME program of the DTI, the modular lessons were done online because of the pandemic.	There is difficulty in navigating online in order to successfully apply for the loan, computer illiteracy for others. Internet dependency in applying for loans and for facilitating the business. Feeling of hassle for the process and technical processes on the side of businesswomen.	Internet connectivity-dependent transactions Lack of technical skills to successfully execute activities. Gradual transition of online services from government.

entrepreneurs and the (2) lack of technical skills to navigate online, are common experiences in this group. To start, the encompassing dependency of entrepreneurs on stable Internet connectivity is a major challenge among Filipino women entrepreneurs. DTI eCommerce (2021) observes that, while developed nations do not consider Internet connection as a primary issue of concern in e-commerce activities, the Philippines suffers severe strains in its telecommunication structures, affecting both big businesses and small entrepreneurs. This is true in the case of R5HR, who states that;

> … I depend on the Internet, and [the] Internet nowadays is sporadic, so in times when the Internet is down, I am not able to operate ….

With her business utterly dependent on the Internet for customer contact, cashless payments, and courier deliveries, sporadic Internet connection is detrimental. This can mean canceled orders, angry courier riders, or unprocessed and delayed payments. For R5HR, who lives in a mountainous area with a limited Internet connection, times of storms, Internet provider connectivity problems, and scheduled power outages mean a severe loss of income.

Another serious problem is the lack of basic technical skills to navigate the online space successfully. For R3JB,

> Yes, I really asked for help. I have a child who is an I.T. I asked for help because I really don't know; I am computer illiterate. Even in using the laptop. It was just recently that my child brought me a laptop when our KMME modular classes started.

R3JB shares her struggle as she tries to effectively use the online platform, having only shifted to online business this year after her bakeshop and cafe experienced a heavy loss in sales during the pandemic. Having also availed of the KMME program, a government program for entrepreneurs, she shares her struggle as she learns through electronic modules that should have been taught in conference form if the pandemic had not hit.

As can be seen from her experience, government transactions are gradually shifting to online as demanded by pandemic restrictions. The application is purely online for the DTI Bayanihan CARES program that gives out no-interest loans to entrepreneurs. In this shift of medium, the other respondents have taken the issue that the process creates hassle and demands much technical skill for a successful application. In the words of RB1FB (Table 1.10),

> True, even for me, I find it a hassle because I have to upload, picture, and scan the ITR and other activities of the same nature.

Online Government Programs and Online Business Income

Finally, it has been observed that the women entrepreneurs were unaware of these government programs in the first place. R4MS recalls that;

> Even if the DTI posts on Facebook, they are many people who remain unaware of the program. Because some sellers don't make it a habit of checking the DTI page, they don't tap it. Because they think that the DTI cannot help anyway.

Table 1.10 Challenges in the Digitized Set-Up (Part 3)

Formulated Meanings	Theme Clusters	Emergent Theme
The respondent feels that some sellers are unaware of the programs of DTI that they post online. Some may also feel that DTI cannot help them as online sellers. The respondent recognizes that the income in her online business is just breakeven.	Receiving that income generated for online business is just breakeven compared to the targeted income needed for long term goals. During the pandemic, the government is slowly transitioning its programs online, making citizen-government transactions digital.	Generates only breakeven income. Lack of online information dissemination of government programs.

As R2CN states,

> And then, it is not much, but at least I have something additional to my income." And in which R3JB agrees; "The fact is, my current income is just break-even even after I shifted online, my income is just enough, because of the situation today. Because no matter how you present your business to people, money is tight right now.

Thus, despite the positive perception of online businesses and the income it generates for the entrepreneurs themselves and the community, there is an urgent need for support for women entrepreneurs, especially in equipping them with the necessary skills to be able to navigate the digitized market successfully. Problems with telecommunications quality are also beyond the scope of individual entrepreneurs, who are completely dependent on the reliable services of Internet companies to be able operate their businesses and generate income. Also, while the government has matched the pace of the times in digitizing its services, its information dissemination efforts and the accessibility of its online programs remain problematic at best.

Suppose that DTI truly believes its recent statement that women-led micro, small, and medium entrepreneurs are crucial in the Philippines' post-COVID-19 recovery, as stated by DTI Secretary Lopez (2021). In that case, it should put its effort into addressing the challenges enumerated above and improving its online services and programs. In giving women entrepreneurs a share of the burden on the economy's post-pandemic recovery, the Philippine government must be an active ally every step of the way.

Conclusion

The state's economic response to the COVID-19 pandemic's effect on Filipino-owned businesses, while existing, is found to be limited in terms of its reach and accessibility. For those who did not avail the government services and programs, entering into online businesses has become a logical step given the current pandemic restrictions. Start-up and established women entrepreneurs facilitate their business online, with, fortunately, little to no challenges encountered in terms of economic, cultural, and social dimensions in their experiences.

However, their lack of basic technical skills and sporadic Internet connection becomes an obstacle that creates a serious loss of income in some situations. To top it off, they also have to employ various marketing strategies to keep their businesses afloat and compete with the intense competition in e-commerce. Succinctly put, Filipino women entrepreneurs have a lot of challenges to deal with, the majority of which they cannot individually address, given the scale of the solution needed.

Recommendations

To ensure stabilization and recovery post-COVID-19, the researchers, therefore, propose the ICT-GAD framework. Actions that ensure business continuity, as well as the means to re-activate business activity and build long-term resilience, are key (Figure 1.1).

I – *Improving the quality of telecommunication services.* This will be one of the many main challenges that the government must consider in supporting women online entrepreneurs. A stable and accessible Internet connection is an essential factor for them to maximize the earning potential of e-commerce platforms fully. This will require the government to invest in affordable ICT infrastructures to make it accessible to the women online business stakeholders, which is only a part of other societal sectors that need a quality Internet connection to function.

C – *Connect women entrepreneurs to accessible avenues for digital learning.* Another challenge identified in this study is the women entrepreneur's lack of basic technical skills to navigate the online space for digital business transactions and to apply for or virtually participate in government programs. An essential element in empowering women

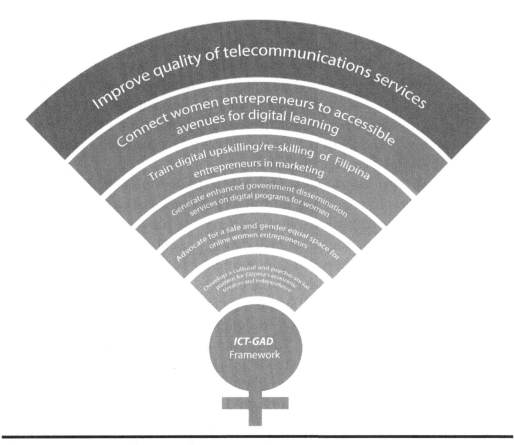

Figure 1.1   ICT-GAD framework.

entrepreneurs is to give them the means so that they will be able to facilitate their online business with little to no help from others, as of the experience of the respondents interviewed in this study.

T – *Train Filipina Entrepreneurs through Digital Upskilling/Reskilling in Marketing.* As a result of the trend where Filipino women entrepreneurs acquired both online and technical skills that boosted their online business sales and customer reach, it is recommended therefore that Filipino businesswomen should be provided with upskilling and reskilling programs through online training courses involving the use of technology and digital platforms which targets on improving digital entrepreneurship and their e-commerce marketing. Through this course of action, Filipino businesswomen will be equipped with new and enhanced digital skills, which are essential to meet the demands of the rapidly evolving business landscape, especially in the new normal.

G – *Generate enhanced government dissemination services on digital programs for women.* The Department of Trade must collaborate with both agencies of ICT and women to ensure the information on their financial and entrepreneurial programs is effectively conveyed to the target sector. This includes a wider reach by government agencies' online pages and covers productive communication among the sectors highlighting all the aspects they must look into: economic, social, political, digital, personal, and mental.

A – *Advocate for a safe and gender-equal space for online women entrepreneurs.* To create and nurture communities of women digital entrepreneurs, a safe space, whether it may be physical or digital, should be attained. This recommendation presents the sad reality which challenges women's freedom of movement. Hence, gender-responsive planning should be considered that ensures female entrepreneurs move freely for them to access public urban and virtual spaces safely.

D – *Develop a cultural and psycho-social pattern for Filipina's Economic Freedom and Independence.* The economic phenomenon that women are leading the economies to recovery termed "she-cession" heavily contributes to reshaping Filipino traditional culture and psycho-social thinking. Women, employees, and students should be encouraged to reach their full potential in their business capability on online platforms. One way of establishing this can be individual-initiated or state-led programs on mental health support and professional business advice during the economic pandemic struggle.

References

Alampay, E. A. (2008). Filipino entrepreneurs on the Internet: When social networking websites meet mobile commerce. *Science, Technology and Society*, 13(2), 211–231.

Balikbayan Media Center. (2021). DTI, Small Business Corporation Approve Over 20,000 Loans for MSMEs. Retrieved from https://balikbayanmagazine.com/business/the-economy/ dti-small-business-corporation-approve-over-20000-loans-for-msmes/

Bartik, A. et al. (2020). The impact of COVID-19 on small business outcomes and expectations. National Academy of Sciences. Retrieved from https://doi. org/10.1073/pnas.2006991117

Cherie Blair Foundation for Women. (2021). Women Entrepreneurs: Surviving the Pandemic and Beyond. 2020 Audit of Women Entrepreneurs in Low and

Middle Income Countries. Retrieved from https://cherieblairfoundation.org/annual-audit-2020/

Cooper, A. C., & Dunkelberg, W. C. (1987). Entrepreneurial research: Old questions, new answers, and methodological issues. *American Journal of Small Business*, 11(3), 11–24. https://doi.org/10.1177/104225878701100301

Dattani, K. (2020). 'Rethinking Social Reproduction in the Time of COVID-19', *Journal of Australian Political Economy*, 85, 51–6.

Department of Trade and Industry (2018). Region 7 - Regional Profile. Retrieved from https://www.dti.gov.ph/regions/region-7/profile/

DTI eCommerce. (2021). DTI | Basta E-Commerce MADALI | eCommerce Philippines 2022 Roadmap. Retrieved from https://ecommerce.dti.gov.ph/madali/environment_roadmap.html#covid

Ken Research. (2021). Increasing Internet Penetration Coupled with Changing Consumer Preference for Online Shopping Expected to Drive the Philippines E-Commerce Logistics Market: Ken Research. GlobeNewswire NewsRoom. Retrieved from https://bit.ly/43qrVgs

Kuek, S. C., Paradi-Guilford, C. M., Fayomi, T., Imaizumi, S., & Ipeirotis, P. (2015). *The Global Opportunity in Online Outsourcing*. World Bank Group. Retrieved from https://openknowledge.worldbank.org/bitstream/handle/10986/22284/The0global0opp0n0online0outsourcing.pdf

Lopez, R. (2021). *Women Entreps Crucial in PH Pandemic Recovery: DTI Chief*. Philippine News Agency. Retrieved from https://www.pna.gov.ph/articles/1133080

McNulty, E. (2020). Leading through Covid-19. MIT Sloan Management Review. Retrieved from https://sloanreview.mit.edu/article/leading-through-covid-19/

Mustafa, F., Khursheed, A., Fatima, M., & Rao, M. (2021). Exploring the impact of COVID-19 pandemic on women entrepreneurs in Pakistan. *International Journal of Gender and Entrepreneurship*, 13(2), 187–203. https://doi.org/10.1108/IJGE-092020-0149

Pena, I. (2002). Intellectual capital and business start-up success. *Journal of Intellectual Capital. Bayanihan CARES | Small Business Corporation*. Sbcorp.gov.ph. Retrieved from https://sbcorp.gov.ph/programs-and-services/bayanihan-cares/

Pihie, Z. A. L., & Bagheri, A. (2010). Entrepreneurial attitude and entrepreneurial efficacy of technical secondary school students. *Journal of Vocational Education and Training*, 62(3), 351–366.

Praveena, K. R., & Sasikumar, S. (2021). Application of Colaizzi's method of data analysis in phenomenological research. *Medico Legal Update*, 21(2), 914–918.

Yandug, J. S. G., De Francia, D. M. B., & Paulo, J. O. (2020). Assessment and Improvement of Facebook Business Platforms for SMEs in the Philippines. Proceedings of the International Conference on Industrial Engineering and Operations Management, Dubai, UAE, March 10-12, 2020. IEOM Society International, Retrieved from http://www.ieomsociety.org/ieom2020/papers/363.pdf

Yukongdi, V., & Cañete, J. M. (2020). The influence of family, human, social capital & government support services on women entrepreneurial start-up decisions: A qualitative study. *Review of Integrative Business and Economics Research*, 9, 307–318.

Ziebland, S., & McPherson, A. (2006). Making sense of qualitative data analysis: An introduction with illustrations from DIPEx (personal experiences of health and illness). *Medical Education*, 40(5), 405–414.

Chapter 2

TikToking, WhatsApping, and Facebooking Agriculture: How Women Are Restructuring Agricultural Value Chains

Richard Boateng

University of Ghana Business School, University of Ghana,
P O Box LG 78, Legon, Ghana

John Serbe Marfo

School of Business, Kwame Nkrumah University of Science and
Technology, P. O. Box Up 1279, KNUST, Kumasi, Ghana

Joseph Budu

School of Technology, Ghana Institute of Management and Public
Administration, Ghana, P. O. Box AH50 Achimota, Ghana

Obed Kwame Adzaku Penu and Edward Entee

University of Ghana Business School, University of Ghana,
P O Box LG 78, Legon, Ghana

Pasty Asamoah

School of Business, Kwame Nkrumah University of Science and
Technology, P. O. Box Up 1279, KNUST, Kumasi, Ghana

DOI: 10.4324/9781003302346-2

Contents

Introduction

Social media can be broadly defined as software-based digital technologies providing users access to digital environments where they can send or receive digital content via an online social network (Kapoor et al., 2018). These technologies are typically displayed as applications (apps) and websites that can be accessed from mobile devices or desktops. Well-known examples of such websites and apps include Facebook, Instagram, Twitter (Appel et al., 2020), and TikTok (Xu et al., 2019).

Alongside enabling people to communicate in everyday situations, social media also plays an important role in entrepreneurship. However, although social media has been reported to contribute to improving women's livelihoods (Beninger et al., 2016; Francesca et al., 2017; Hossain & Rahman, 2018), little is known about the impact of social media on female entrepreneurship. The lack of knowledge in this field has led to a call for more research on women's agency and empowerment through social media (Masika & Bailur, 2015).

In this body of research, women's empowerment is understood as a woman's ability to create value from social media within the agricultural value chain.

This chapter investigates female entrepreneurs' social media-enhanced experiences with the agricultural value chain in a developing country. More specifically, we recount the results of two qualitative case studies on female digital entrepreneurs whose trade in online vegetable and rice retailing in Ghana involves the use of the "TikTok", WhatsApp, and Facebook messaging platforms.

We aim to understand how women leverage digital opportunities afforded to them by social media using these platforms and the conditions that shape these affordances. The next two sections present the case studies. This is followed by several possible reflections that could be construed from our results. Finally, the concluding section outlines several questions we believe to be worth exploring in future research.

Case A: KayaApp Grocery – An Online Vegetable Retail Business

Overview

KayaApp grocery (KG) is an agribusiness specializing in the retailing of fresh vegetables and other foodstuffs to individuals and organizations in Kumasi and other parts of Ghana. The tagline of the company is "Shop for more with less". The shop operates by buying fresh foodstuff and vegetables and selling them to its customers. This retail business, owned by Naomi K, was launched in February 2020. The impetus for its creation was a random video that Naomi posted on TikTok. The post quickly went viral, receiving over 30,000 views overnight. The video in the post described how friends pooled their resources together, bought a box of tomatoes, and shared them equally among themselves. Two months after the viral video appeared on TikTok, the business grew into a large group over different platforms hosting several groups in various regions. Currently, there is a group on Facebook with over 5,300 followers. KG also has different WhatsApp groups for customers located in different regions of Ghana.

Currently, there are WhatsApp groups for Accra, Kumasi, Takoradi, Koforidua, Tema, and other parts of Ghana, with each group consisting of more than 200 customers. Naomi describes her business as follows (Figure 2.1):

> We are a digital grocery business that runs foodstuff errands in Kumasi and other parts of Ghana. We use social media to get customers food items at a cheaper cost.

Figure 2.1   KayaApp TikTok page. (Source: Fieldwork Data.)

KG's physical retail shop is in Racecourse, a suburb of Kumasi in the Ashanti region. The Racecourse area is a bustling city center which serves as a transport hub and a market of perishable and non-perishable products. Trading in this city center market is fundamentally premised on hard bargaining. KG's location enables the business to have access to fresh vegetables and foodstuff and easy transportation links to various parts of Kumasi and beyond. For Accra and Tema customers, KG delivery is only on Thursdays through STC, a state-owned transport company, where a carriage in the bus is reserved for KG to transport its products to customers in Accra at a special cost. For other regions, there are arrangements with various bus conductors, station masters, and drivers.

Transporting products in this way ensures that KG's goods are delivered fresh to their customers. Once the products reach the destination region, customers make their own pick-up arrangements. KG does not offer door-to-door delivery. According to Naomi, some of her customers have arranged for Bolt or Uber drivers to pick their purchases up. Kumasi has a different arrangement whereby products are delivered to customers' homes by tricycles.

Naomi describes herself as a social media enthusiast and spends long hours on different social media platforms every day. Beyond the KG business, Naomi works as a researcher and trainer in digital marketing.

Naomi claims she has taught digital marketing skills to over 80 people from various backgrounds and of different social statuses. She conducts monthly trainings in different parts of Ghana.

Along with her formal employment as a digital marketing consultant, Naomi reports earning about 20% of her monthly income from operating KayaApp, which is estimated to have a value of $1,200.00.

How Social Media Drives Value in KG

Engaging Buyers and Facilitating Transactions and Deliveries

KG gained popularity in 2020 when the COVID-19 pandemic was in full swing and when a national lockdown was in place. Naomi describes how she started:

> Everyone who knows me is aware that I am always on different social media platforms during the day, especially TikTok. During the lockdown of the pandemic, I noticed that foodstuff was difficult to come to while prices were quite high. One day, I recorded a video post on TikTok on food stuff and vegetables that I chanced upon. These foodstuffs and vegetables were cheap and plenty. So, in the video, I asked who would join me so that we contribute, buy them in bulk, and then share. The idea was that buying bulk foodstuff and vegetables means lower prices. The post had over 30,000 views overnight. Interestingly, I had tons of messages from my followers in the various regions willing to become part of my call. Thereafter, I grouped them into regions, for example, those in Accra became Kaya BBS Accra.

Naomi further explains that products and prices are advertised in online groups on Tuesdays. Any member interested in the week's Bulk Buy and Share (BBS) idea sends payments via mobile by the end of Tuesday. For her customers located in Accra, dispatch is performed on Thursdays through a local transport company, and collection is on the same day at bus terminals. This mode of dispatch ensures that the customers receive fresh vegetables. Pick-ups in Accra and Tema are at the customer's own cost and risk.

The Kaya BBS uses social media to engage and interact directly with customers, thus skipping intermediaries such as traditional market queens.

Market queens in Ghana are democratically elected traders' representatives trading in a certain product or product group (Clark, 1994). For example, in any given market, for products including tomatoes and yam, there would be the so-called Tomatoes Market Queen and Yam Market Queen. Market queens ensure that the products that they oversee flow smoothly into the traditional commodity market. Market queens hold power from their members and traditional authorities like chiefs who superintend markets through market queens. In the Ashanti region, for instance, all market queens submit the produce to a specific sub-chief at the Manhyia palace, the seat of the King of the Ashanti Kingdom. Market queens would collect the produce from various market women within their product grouping and submit it quarterly (3 months) to the sub-chief responsible for them at the Manhyia palace for further use as the traditional authorities deem fit. In addition, on festive occasions such as Akwasidae Kese (a grand festival celebrated by the Ashanti Kingdom), market queens and women in their product groupings collect some of their products and present them as gifts to traditional authorities through the sub-chief designated to manage their affairs in the markets.

The Five "S"s of Social Media Value Creation Activities

KG is present on Facebook, TikTok, and WhatsApp. Naomi believes that her business' presence on various social media platforms enables more effective customer acquisition and communication opportunities at a cheaper cost. As Naomi explains, "the use of social media in my business exposes the business and its operations to diverse customers in different locations at almost zero cost". There are five main activities that KG performs on different social media platforms. Other activities used to complement these five main activities are conducted outside social media.

- **Building the social community,** which entails building KG's social media pages. This includes specifying how potential community members could join a specific group (see Figure 2.2). KG uses this activity to increase its customer pool and to promote its mode of operation.
- **Social publishing,** whereby KG brands its content, advertises, and shares perceived valuable content across various groups. Figure 2.3 shows KG advertising vegetables to group members through WhatsApp.

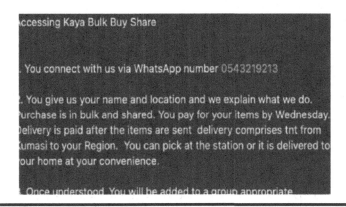

Figure 2.2   Snapshot demonstrating the "Building the social community" activity. (Source: Fieldwork Data.)

- **Social commerce,** which includes a call to action, buying and selling, servicing customers, and managing existing customers.
- **Social logistics,** which includes managing customers' order requests, order fulfillment, packaging, transportation, and delivery.
- **Social customer experience,** which includes following up with customers to obtain feedback, addressing challenges, and ensuring customer satisfaction with KayaApp. This activity aims to create a lasting positive impression with the social media service across the entire customer journey.

Figure 2.3   KayaApp grocery advertising to group members through WhatsApp. (Source: Fieldwork Data.)

Value Creation Process – Disintermediation of Service Providers

At the center of KG, there is an actor who operates and integrates various available resources, guided by mechanisms of beliefs and norms, to create value. However, value is not created by a single actor, i.e., KG, but rather by a network of multiple actors whose mutual engagement and exchange of resources is partly enabled and driven by social media. An actor's link to other actors is through the network and the embedded service. Accordingly, KayaApp's dynamic system of actors can be decomposed into the following two components: (1) social participants (i.e., customers) and (2) economic market participants (i.e., service providers). The actors can be further sub-categorized into customers, service providers, and the facilitator (KayaApp) (Figure 2.4).

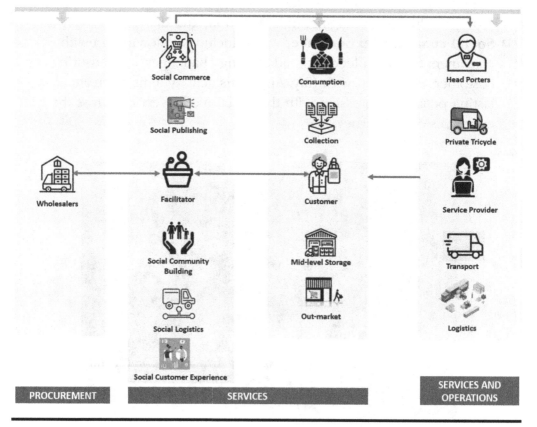

Figure 2.4   KayaApp value chain downstream activities. (Source: Fieldwork Data.)

Behaviors Observed in the KayaApp Grocery Value Chain

The value chain created by KG is characterized by three main behaviors of the actors involved: governance, social capital, and social networks.

KG uses modular governance, which typically involves customization of products and services. Although KG's model does not involve interactions between final consumers and farmers or wholesalers/market queens, KG consumers acquire specific products in bulk, or in necessary quantities, with their available budget.

Another type of governance observed in the KG model is captive governance. In this respect, KG largely depends on the strong relationship between the business and the buyers as facilitated by social media. These buyers are organized in closed local WhatsApp groups. This ensures that, despite being few, group members hold power and can control what they buy from the market and how much they pay for these goods.

The second behavior is social capital, i.e., the relationships between the members of the KayaApp BBS. These relationships are premised on common interests – in this case, the desire to bulk buy foodstuff and vegetables and share these at a bargain cost. KG's value chain aims to bridge social capital through the uniting of group members, despite their different backgrounds, in collective action and in their desire to obtain information regarding the quality and price of vegetables. The unity of a group is also facilitated by the combined transportation of foodstuff and vegetables to common destinations where each group resides. Interaction between members and facilitator creates a special trust which encourages buyers to feel they can safely send their money before KG sends out the orders. This has become possible through the trustful relationships between customers and KG.

The third behavior is social networking among the actors. In terms of centrality, the facilitator (KG) has the most ties in the value chain. The KG business has ties to market queens/wholesalers, to different entities that provide service to it, and to end-customers. In contrast, some service providers have a direct relationship link only with the facilitator, while actors in transportation have two relationship links (i.e., with the facilitator and customers).

Case B – Mackeli Processing – An Online Rice Retailer

Overview and Business Start-Up

Mackeli processing is a social media-based family business that sources and sells local Ghanaian rice by leveraging Facebook and WhatsApp. Mark and Kekeli, husband and wife, respectively, found a new likeable taste for local Ghanaian rice. As they purchased and consumed their new delicacy, they observed how the COVID-19 lockdown restrictions made it difficult for families to procure and store food items. Kekeli notes that "We picked the signals from social media; there were groups that started like Asigame – people were putting items out there for sale, especially foodstuffs, hence we contacted Maame Yaa, a farmer friend in Asutuare, a town in the Eastern Region of Ghana, who agreed to supply us with our preferred variety of local Ghanaian rice. Thereafter, we went for our first ten bags of local rice from Asutuare to test the market".

Further, she recounts how they designed a flier and shared it online to attract leads and eventual sales. She said, "we designed and shared fliers in a WhatsApp group we created for the members of our church. We basically used Facebook and WhatsApp, and informed our friends also to share their status, and we took advantage of our church social media platforms and other group platforms that we belong to".

The first week's ten bags sold out. They went for another ten bags, which also sold out. Kekeli intimated that they "then created a Facebook page, did some jingles about how healthy it is to eat local rice, the fiber content, and why you should choose to eat healthily". Further, they "will occasionally boost the page, and people will contact us". Interestingly, the advertisements started catching on, so "the very first people who consumed started giving us referrals, and that is how we started getting into the market gradually to get people on board", Kekeli shares with a smile. She wonders whether people have stopped using mobile SMS; because she observed that orders came mostly through WhatsApp. Even, pre-sale and after-sale communication also came via WhatsApp or sometimes Facebook. In addition to the social media activities, they also targeted corporate institutions because they realized they also needed this variety of local rice. This offline targeting also paid off. Mark, in sharing some of the results, mentioned that "sometimes in a week, we can supply like five bags, which expanded to ten, and it was going in that direction" (Figure 2.5).

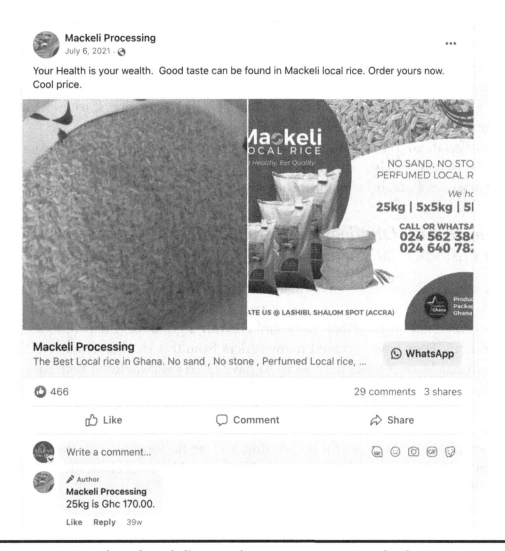

Figure 2.5 Snapshot of Mackeli processing engagement on Facebook. (Source: Fieldwork Data.)

Linking Social Media to Value-Driven Activities

Consequently, they [Kekeli and Mark] linked their Facebook advertisement's call-to-action to WhatsApp. Kekeli intimated that "when we do some of the boosting, we link the Facebook Ad to WhatsApp, so when the enquiries come, they go straight to our WhatsApp". More importantly, they ensured that they matched the referrals and increasing demand with high-quality rice, especially because of their clientele's demographics – educated, employed, and largely engaged in their work activities. They intimate that "… because we don't have a store, having our clients refer or recommend us is very important to us". They created a virtuous cycle of attraction, purchasing, and referral early on to keep a steady stream of customer orders whose fulfillment created satisfaction. To ensure consistent client satisfaction with the quality of rice delivered, they consistently solicited feedback to improve on any identified shortfalls. Kekeli explains that "when people buy, we WhatsApp them to find out how they felt about the quality, the taste and all that. So, when we also use their feedback, we ask permission from them, take a screenshot, and use it to promote the business further".

Defined Value Offering: Product Quality and Customer Satisfaction

This dogged focus on product quality and customer satisfaction has brought Mackeli Local Rice to a point where "previous consumers will just tag when somebody asks on Facebook to be linked with a good local rice vendor or source". They have received many orders from this mechanism as well. Unfortunately, over time, they seem to have been overwhelmed with the number of orders because they do not have enough rice to meet the ever-increasing demand. Kekeli laments that "because we don't have the capacity to stock more and because we are interested in a particular variety which our supplier is able to get for us on time, we are no longer doing the (Facebook ad) boosting because we will not be able to meet the demand and that might give us a negative social media image. It's very difficult to correct a bad image about yourself".

Gains from Social Capital

Even without marketing aggressively as before, Mark reveals that "we still get customers who tell us that 'I saw this on Facebook' and I sometimes begin to wonder, but I didn't boost, I didn't promote, but how am I still getting calls from them … people are sharing, and people are liking, and that's where we are getting the customers from". He attributes such sales enquiries to unceasing referrals from satisfied clients. Currently, as he further intimates, "our promotion and boosting are on a low budget, but we are still getting referrals and recommendations and sharing on social media. We even found that somebody has shared our flier on Home Garden (a popular Facebook group on agriculture and nutrition), so that should tell you that people are doing the work on behalf".

Customer Data Matters – Collect as You Build Social Capital

Despite having a low advertising budget, Kekeli and Mark are still building and capitalizing on social capital. Mark boasts of how the couple has "this very nice relationship with clients", and explains why they need to maintain it. He said, "the focus is to build a good clientele base because we know that the future of the rice business is very promising, and it's the star of the future so that in the future, we can supply the quantity that the customers will demand. Because we know that the future is good, we are collecting the data on the customers and building the clientele base so that in the future, we can contact them".

Revenue Generated

This side business, as the couple describes it, is generating about 20% of the family income. Kekeli mentions that "as a researcher, and my husband a hotelier, I can say that we are generating about 20–30% of our family income from this local rice business". Mark, in giving some confirmation, shared that "in the beginning, we spent about $5 per 25kg bag, and brought 20 bags; we were making $5 profit per bag. Currently (in December 2022), we spend $37 per 25kg bag. As the price of food in general, and that of rice in particular, skyrockets, there is room to make more revenue because demand would not seem to end anytime soon".

Further, social media indirectly reduces their operational costs, such as shop rentals and paying the wages of a salesperson or caretaker. Kekeli, who doubles as the financial manager, intimated that "we can also say that when you look at the cost of renting a shop, paying a salesperson, social media tends to offer a cheaper option to running the business. As of now, we are getting customer data, … at most we boost our Facebook page, and we're good to go. It doesn't cost so much, so it helps us minimise our marketing and operational costs in general".

Challenges Faced

Mackeli processing has two primary challenges. First, sourcing from only one specific processor (miller). There is a somewhat reverse captive governance relationship between the processor and this social media-based company. The processor refuses to give them any link to producers or farmers that grow the variant and the quality of rice purchased. The processor controls supply and is sometimes unable to meet the increasing demand received from social media customers readily. On occasions where the company had purchased from other processors, their customers rejected the produce – due to differences in quality and taste – and they had to do a recall. Hence, they "feel" tied to the processor.

Second, the company has limited storage space – one of their rooms has been converted to storage, and they have ceased providing small, packaged quantities of rice (e.g., 5 kg) and are focusing on large packaged quantities (25 kg) for sale. Due to this, they cannot scale up geographically and actively supply to other regions beyond Accra.

Reflections from the Case Studies

This section offers reflections which can serve as guidelines for researchers studying how female digital entrepreneurs in the agricultural value chains can create value using social media.

■ Women are motivated to use social media to make use of avenues for building digital businesses.
■ Female entrepreneurs' digital skills – including knowledge of social media – contribute to women's sustained use of social media to create value for their digital businesses.
■ Social media enable female entrepreneurs to advertise different packages available for subscription to their clients and to engage and interact with their customers directly, thereby reducing interference from intermediaries.
■ Using social media enables female entrepreneurs to leverage opportunities in customer acquisition and communication, all at a cheaper cost, as customers from very distant locations can be reached at almost zero cost.
■ In both case studies, social media has somewhat created value in the following five ways: (1) building the social community, (2) social publishing, (3) social commerce, (4) social logistics, and (5) social customer experience.
■ With social media, value is created not only by the business but also through a network of multiple actors whose mutual engagement and exchange of resources are partly enabled and driven by social media.

Questions for Discussion for Cases A and B

To analyze the impact of social media on female digital entrepreneurs in the agricultural value chain, the following questions can be discussed by students or practitioners:

1. How are female digital entrepreneurs using social media? What social media features or functions are being leveraged by female digital entrepreneurs?
2. How are female digital entrepreneurs able to use social media, as demonstrated in the case studies? What skills do they tend to possess to make these forms of use possible?
3. What conditions in the agricultural value chains make the identified social media features or functions relevant to these entrepreneurs?
4. What livelihood outcomes are experienced or obtained by female digital entrepreneurs in the agricultural value chain?
5. Is social media enough to create value in the online retailing of agricultural produce?

Acknowledgement

We would like to thank Caribou Digital who provided financial support and mentoring for this case study as part of a broader study on Social Agriculture in Ghana. Without their contributions, this project would not have been possible.

References

Appel, G., Grewal, L., Hadi, R., & Stephen, A. T. (2020). The future of social media in marketing. *Journal of the Academy of Marketing Science*, *48*(1), 79–95. https://doi.org/10.1007/s11747-019-00695-1

Beninger, S., Ajjan, H., Mostafa, R. B., & Crittenden, V. L. (2016). A road to empowerment: Social media use by women entrepreneurs in Egypt. *International Journal of Entrepreneurship and Small Business*, *27*(2–3), 308–332.

Clark, G. (1994). *Onions Are My Husband: Survival and Accumulation by West African Market Women*. Chicago, IL: University of Chicago Press.

Francesca, M. C., Paola, D., & Paola, P. (2017). Women in business and social media: Implications for female entrepreneurship in emerging countries.

African Journal of Business Management, 11(14), 316–326. https://doi.org/10.21043/iqtishadia.v14i2.9483

Hossain, M., & Rahman, M. F. (2018). Social media and the creation of entrepreneurial opportunity for women. *Management, 8*(4), 99–108. https://doi.org/10.5923/j.mm.20180804.02

Kapoor, K. K., Tamilmani, K., Rana, N. P., Patil, P., Dwivedi, Y. K., & Nerur, S. (2018). Advances in social media research: Past, present and future. *Information Systems Frontiers, 20*(3), 531–558. https://doi.org/10.1007/s10796-017-9810-y

Masika, R., & Bailur, S. (2015). Negotiating women's agency through ICTs: A comparative study of Uganda and India. *Gender, Technology and Development, 19*(1), 43–69. https://doi.org/10.1177/0971852414561615

Xu, L., Yan, X., & Zhang, Z. (2019). Research on the causes of the "TikTok" app becoming popular and the existing problems. *Journal of Advanced Management Science, 7*(2), 59–63.

Chapter 3

Digitalization of Business Operations and Empowerment of Female Entrepreneurs

Janet Serwah Boateng
School for Development Studies, University of Cape Coast, Cape Coast, Ghana

Mavis Serwah Benneh Mensah and Isaac Kosi
School of Business, University of Cape Coast, Cape Coast, Ghana

Sabina Appiah-Boateng
School for Development Studies, University of Cape Coast, Cape Coast, Ghana

Martin Boakye Osei
Department of People and Organizations, Bournemouth University, Poole, England

Contents

DOI: 10.4324/9781003302346-3

Introduction

Digitalization of business operations is fast gaining ground on the ticket
of massive developments in information and communication technology
(ICT), the Internet of Things (IoT) and, in recent times, the importance of
upgrading offline operations into online activities due to the 2019 Corona
Virus pandemic (COVID-19). The pandemic is said to have affected millions of
businesses worldwide through limited human movement and contacts, leading
to reduced investments, sales, and profitability and business closures (Elam
et al., 2021; Shen et al., 2020). According to the 2020 World Economic Forum
report on the Future of Jobs, 84% of employers are said to digitalize working
processes, while the unemployed emphasize acquiring digital skills.

The report further notes that globally, between 62% and 90% of businesses
in 14 sectors, including agriculture, food and beverage (80%), manufacturing
(82%), and financial services (90%), are likely to adopt e-commerce and digital
trade by 2025. These developments indicate the pivotal role of digitalization
of business operations for survival, growth and development (Elam et al.,
2021). This chapter demonstrates that digitalization is equally important to the
empowerment of female entrepreneurs, specifically in the domain of their
personal and psychological empowerment, relational empowerment, and
economic empowerment (Alkhaled & Berglund, 2018; Kabeer, 2020).

Researchers and practitioners acknowledge that entrepreneurship is a critical
tool for women empowerment and for realizing the Sustainable Development
Goals (SDGs) (Foss et al., 2019; Williams & Kedir, 2018). However, female
entrepreneurs battle with numerous peculiar challenges that hold back their
empowerment and the attainment of the SDGs. Feminist theories, grounded

in addressing gender discrimination, offer comprehensive insights into the challenges from various angles. For instance, the liberal feminist theory highlights unequal and limited access to resources, while the feminist standpoint theories analyze socio-cultural and structural impediments to women's advancement (Hekman, 1997; Marlow, 2020). Research shows that these drawbacks confine most female entrepreneurs to practice entrepreneurship in low-income sectors. That includes subsistence agriculture, retail trade, and care work and are saddled with a small customer base, infrastructural and growth challenges, and a high failure rate (Boohene, 2009; Foss et al., 2019).

In recognition of digitalization power solutions to those obstacles, the 2020/2021 Women's Entrepreneurship report emphasizes its crucial role in expanding market focus and growth of women's enterprises (Elam et al., 2021). Nevertheless, existing research accounts for less of this phenomenon. As an emerging research field, there is a deficit of insights into the forms of transactional digital platforms and services that women entrepreneurs, especially in developing countries in Africa, use and the extent to which this form of digitalization drives the personal and psychological, relational, and economic empowerment of these entrepreneurs. As a result, this study aimed to analyze the use of digital platforms and services in business transactions and the empowerment of female entrepreneurs in Ghana.

The chapter reviews related literature in the next section. Next is the methodology, results and discussions, conclusions and recommendations, and practical and managerial implications.

Literature Review

The review discusses the theoretical framework and the concepts of digitalization and empowerment. It further builds on the theoretical and conceptual review to develop the study's hypotheses.

Theoretical Framework

This chapter draws on the liberal feminist theory and the feminist standpoint theories to project digitalization as a potential resource for the empowerment of female entrepreneurs. Foss et al. (2019) note that the liberal feminist theory regards gender as equivalent to sex, hence the use of the binaries men and women as explanatory variables in research contrary to the post-structuralist feminist theoretical stand that considers gender as socially constructed. Just like all other forms of feminism, the two theories acknowledge discrimination against females, and for that matter women, in all spheres of life as a bane to their socioeconomic advancement. As a result, feminists underscore female empowerment as a critical tool for addressing the disempowerment of females which arises from gender discrimination and female subordination (Hekman, 1997; Marlow, 2020).

The conceptualization of the feminist debate has gained recognition and acceptance within the gender and development literature as an important theoretical perspective that advocates for the inclusion of gender in development (GAD) programming (Omilusi, 2017). Boateng et al. (2021) reiterated Ihalainen et al. (2020)'s suggestions that the rethinking of women and development (WAD) issues, across Africa and the world, is projected to draw on feminist theories to correspond through the assimilation of women's issues into development, using women-in-development (WID) approach. Additionally, this chapter recognizes the relevance of WAD and GAD to women's empowerment.

Proponents of WAD, just like the socialist feminists, believe that women's subordination in society occurs because of the development of private properties and capitalism WAD proponents were mostly Marxist feminists who advocated for the abolition of private property, but ignored the nature of gender inequality, gender relations and the challenges women face in society (Boateng, 2017). Some feminists and development practitioners critiqued the two schools of thought and indicated that neither WID nor WAD adequately addressed the causes of gender inequality in society.

Consequently, GAD explains further how women could be empowered. The GAD theory demonstrates advocates' concerns about women's subordination and the various efforts regarding proposals and the promulgations of concepts and approaches to deal with the societal structures that tend to disadvantage women (Boateng, 2017). Similar to the liberal feminist view, which argues that institutional adjustments and policy shifts are necessary to open up traditional male-dominated areas (Ahl & Marlow, 2012), the GAD approach proposes empowering women to break through the male-dominated space, including entrepreneurship and politics. The digital space has been an open platform, and empowered women could compete to enhance their socioeconomic well-being.

In order for women to tap into opportunities such as those offered by digitalization, proponents of the liberal feminist theory proffer equal rights and equal access to resources for both sexes, whereas the feminist standpoint theorists, particularly the radicalists and the socialists, emphasize the removal of capitalists and patriarchal oppression, respectively, for example, through a reversal of social structures (Boohene, 2009; Hekman, 1997; Marlow, 2020). Banda (2006) maintained that extreme inequalities in opportunity directly affect what people can be and what they can do. This is evidenced, for instance, in research by Ali and Shabir (2017) and Williams and Kedir (2018), which demonstrate the capability of women entrepreneurs to perform equally as their male counterparts when given equal access to resources to operate in a fair environment. From these theoretical perspectives, this chapter recognizes digitalization, in terms of the use of digital platforms and services in economic activities, to constitute an essential technological resource for the empowerment of female entrepreneurs.

Digitalization

According to Kuusisto (2017), digitalization is organizations' use of digital assets to improve their performance and the effects of digital technologies on how the world works. It is thus the adaption of a system, or process, to use computers and the internet for business or trading (Tech Target, 2022). It describes the transition from an industrial age characterized by analogue technologies to an era of knowledge and creativity characterized by digital technologies and digital business innovation. Digitalization allows companies to sell goods without their physical presence and reach the digital platform through digitization. Thus, digitization is when products, text, pictures, sounds, and messages are converted into digital format and processed by a computer. The information makes preserving, accessing and sharing easier (Tech Target, 2022). Female entrepreneurs digitize and digitalize many products and economically empower themselves.

According to Briggs (2022), "digital empowerment is what assists organizations in opening up the knowledge, experience, and values that people already have – it is about discovering and releasing the power of your people in a controlled and focussed way" (p. 1). Empowering women digitally in business means they could transform and become more strategic (McKeown & Durkin, 2017). The Ghanaian woman has access to many digital platforms, including Facebook, Twitter, WhatsApp Messenger, Mobile Money Transfer (MOMO), and Short Message Services (SMS). They transact business through digital devices such as phones, desktops, or laptops.

Schillo and Ebrahimi (2022) reiterated Huang et al.'s (2007) argument that a business is considered digital only when its web portal is crucial to business activities and decision-making. The business is carried out mostly through online content and web applications. Through digitization and digitalization, Ghanaian women offer products to customers and clients. Because of customer relationships, they economically and socially empower themselves. Also, doing business effectively on digital platforms and increasing their income empower them financially and politically. Digitally empowering women is not far-fetched as it adds to the revolution of giving them the economic power to transform themselves. Thus, digitally empowering women could economically develop many women (Bhutani & Paliwal, 2015; Chakraborty, 2019; Tsan et al., 2019). Economic development and technological growth create changes in labor markets (Kogiso et al., 2017), and this change in women's life will enhance their choices.

The Concept of Empowerment

Empowerment enables women to realize their identity, potentiality, and power in all spheres of their lives (Prasad, 2014). Thus, the change process, which often begins within the individual and addresses women's needs, is empowerment. One of the central pillars of empowerment is an agency, which correlates to women's ability to make strategic life choices in a situation where this ability was previously denied to them (Tursunova, 2014). Agency is exercised through mobilizing valued resources such as education, economic opportunities, and decision-making positions, which are the means of strength distributed through the various institutions and relationships (Boateng, 2017).

Women's empowerment means giving equal status to women and giving them the capacity and ways to direct their lives toward desired goals (Bhutani & Paliwal, 2015; Chakraborty, 2019). For women to consider themselves to have confidence in whatever they do and access resources to perceive that they can make choices shows that they are empowered (Afshar, 1998). Empowering women has been a catchphrase in the millennial as the concept appeared in the phases of the two global goals: the Millennium Development Goal 3 (gender equality and women empowerment) and the Sustainable Development Goal 5 (gender equality and empowering all women and girls). Therefore, empowering women economically, socially, and politically has been on the agenda of many scholars, as the concept has gained greater awareness (Dejene, 2007), and it is trending in the technological and digitalization period.

Empowering women is a crucial step toward attaining sustainable development on a global scale. Women are a nation's most valuable resource. It is important to acknowledge that women shape and construct a country's future. However, women have less access to power, including less favorable cultural ideals, greater social obligations to uphold, and access to resource management. Numerous areas of daily life, including access to education, job prospects, and economic abilities, exhibit this gender imbalance (United Nations Development Programme [UNDP], 2015). When feminists in the third world became dissatisfied with the predominantly apolitical and economic WID, WAD, and GAD models in development interventions during the 1980s, there were significant critiques and discussions about women's empowerment.

The framework and technique known as empowerment have been developed to overcome inequality (Kabeer, 2001). It means that women have the power to influence how their daily lives are conducted in the social, economic, and political spheres (Bhutani & Paliwal, 2015; Chakraborty, 2019). It is that kind of power which enables them to move from the periphery to the center stage. Sen (1994) defined empowerment as changing the power dynamics that limit the choices and autonomy of women and negatively impact their health and well-being. The definition offered by Batliwala (1994) is explicated in terms of the degree of control individuals have over external actions that affect their welfare. According to Keller and Mbewewe (1991), it is a process whereby women learn to organize themselves in a way that increases their level of independence. It asserts their right to make decisions independently and take charge of the resources necessary to challenge and overcome their subordination.

Kabeer goes beyond these definitions by asserting that empowerment is questioning the status quo and thinking outside the box. He further defines this concept as expanding people's capacity to make wise decisions in situations they had not previously been able to do so (Kabeer, 2001). Theorizing of empowerment places a strong emphasis on two main perspectives: one more individualistic, namely through women's capacities and the right to freedom of expression of personal choice (Kabeer, 1999), and one more collectivistic, namely through collective behavior and adherence to cultural norms that emphasize collective growth (Budgeon, 2015; Kurtiş et al., 2016).

Hypotheses Development

The effects of digitalization on female empowerment occupy a central space in contemporary research on women empowerment. As an emerging field of inquiry, researchers have given attention to topics such as digital platforms use and women empowerment in the health sector (Al Dahdah, 2021; Kontos et al., 2014; Maxwell et al., 2021), in social work and politics (von Dop et al., 2016), and business (Buer et al., 2021; Lal, 2021). Buer et al. (2021)

and Yu et al. (2021) investigated the phenomenon and affirmed its relevance but bemoaned the paucity of research on the subject matter.

While Buer et al. (2021) established a positive digitalization contribution to performance, Yu et al. (2021) found an inverted-u-shaped relationship between the two variables. Yu et al.'s (2021) study further indicated the tendency for enterprises to report negative returns from digitalization when optimized. Similarly, Schillo and Ebrahimi (2022) reported a negative relationship between digitalization and women's access to venture capital funding. Given the mixed results in the literature, this chapter relies on non-directional hypotheses to predict that (*Hypothesis 1 = H₁*):

H_1: Digitalization of business transactions will have a significant effect on the economic empowerment of female entrepreneurs.

Digitalization and the psychological and relational/social empowerment of females in their productive roles have, generally, not been a subject of investigation. Scholars emphasize the importance of the psychological empowerment of females, but ironically, as Miniesy et al. (2021) note, it is often not assessed in empowerment studies. Considering the fact that female empowerment is incomplete without fulfillment of the personal and psychological dimension, we draw on previous research by Alam et al. (2009) and Ye and Yang (2020), which confirmed the importance of digital platform use to the psychological empowerment of females to hypothesize that (*Hypothesis 2 = H₂*):

H_2: Digitalization of business transactions will have a significant positive effect on the personal and psychological empowerment of female entrepreneurs.

Prior research, for example, by Alam et al. (2009) in rural Bangladesh and Ye and Yang (2020) in India, confirmed the positive role of digital platform use in fostering, among other things, social empowerment of women. These studies underscore the likelihood of a positive contribution of digitalization to the social empowerment of female entrepreneurs in the current study, which was conducted in a developing country setting (Ghana) which is quite similar to that of Bangladesh and India. Miniesy et al. (2022) further established in a related study in India that the relational/social empowerment of women entrepreneurs was more evident than the other forms of empowerment. As a result, the third hypothesis of the study is that (*Hypothesis 3 = H₃*):

H_3: Digitalization of business transactions will have a significant positive effect on the relational empowerment of female entrepreneurs.

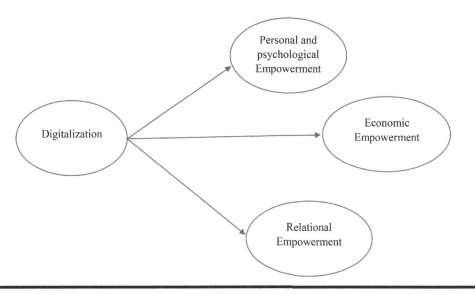

Figure 3.1   Conceptual model.

This chapter's conceptual framework is shown below based on the theoretical and empirical review. We conceptualize that female entrepreneurs' digitalization of business operations will positively influence their personal and psychological, economic, and relational empowerment (Figure 3.1).

Methodology

The quest of this research to analyze the effects of digitalization of business transactions on the empowerment of female entrepreneurs necessitated the adoption of the post-positivist philosophical worldview and the quantitative research approach. Creswell and Creswell (2018) identify the post-positivist research paradigm as an avenue for identifying and assessing the causes that influence outcomes. The literature on digitalization of business operations in Ghana reports entrepreneurs' wide adoption of mobile money services in their business transactions (Penney et al., 2021). However, there is a research gap on female entrepreneurs' use of such services and other digital platforms and the degree to which they advance their empowerment, requiring a survey.

The target population were female entrepreneurs in the Cape Coast Metropolis of Ghana. Due to a high degree of informality and the absence of a comprehensive register of female entrepreneurs in the Metropolis, the accessible population comprised all female entrepreneurs who were available and willing to participate in the study. Through convenience and snowball sampling, 158 female entrepreneurs participated in the cross-sectional survey in August and September 2022. The research participants completed a self-administered questionnaire that sought, among other things, information on the types of digital platforms and services they use in their business transactions, the extent of use, psychological empowerment, social empowerment, and economic empowerment as a result of the user experience.

Mobile money services, social media platforms including WhatsApp, Twitter, and Facebook and online marketing platforms like Jiji and Tonaton were among the platforms that were examined. Kuusisto (2017) defined digitalization as all digital communication technologies, automated systems, and data-storing devices. The study used a seven-point Likert-type scale to measure the digitalization of business operations in terms of the extent of use of the above-mentioned digital platforms in business activities (see Appendix).

The measurement of female empowerment drew upon insights from women empowerment scales by van Dop et al. (2016), specifically on the service user psychological empowerment scale and Lal (2021) on social/relational empowerment and economic empowerment. Eight items constituted the personal and psychological empowerment scale, while the relational and economic empowerment scale had six items each (see Appendix). On a scale of 1 to 7, representing the least extent to a great extent, respondents were asked to rate the degree to which digital platforms and services had empowered them.

A total of 178 questionnaires were retrieved at the end of data collection in September 2022. Screening of the survey questionnaires resulted in the rejection of 20, of which one was scanty. The remaining 19, per the indication of the gender of the respondents, were filled by men and were therefore excluded from the analysis. Descriptive analysis, including frequencies and means, was carried out with the IBM SPSS Version 25, while inferential analysis was conducted with the partial least squares structural equation modeling (PLS-SEM).

Results and Discussions

Respondents' Demographic Characteristics

The study examined the age of respondents, level of education, type of economic activity and years of operation. Most respondents (65%) were under 30 years, while the least (3.8%) were above 50 (Table 3.1). This reflects that most respondents were from the University of Cape

Table 3.1   Respondents' Demographic Characteristics

Variable	Frequency	Percentage
Age		
Below 30 years	102	64.6
30–39 years	30	19.0
40–49 years	19	12.0
50–59 years	5	3.2
60–69 years	1	0.6
Missing values	1	0.6
Total	**158**	**100**
Education		
Never been to school	8	5.1
Basic/Elementary	5	3.2
Secondary	12	7.6
Technical/Vocational	3	1.9
Tertiary	128	81.0
Missing values	2	1.3
Total	**158**	**100**
Business Activity		
Trading	62	39.2
Sewing	18	11.4
Cooking and baking	14	8.9
Manufacturing	10	6.3
Food processing	10	6.3
Service	26	16.5
Farming and aquaculture	11	7.0
Missing values	7	4.4
Total	**158**	**100**

(Continued)

Table 3.1 Respondents' Demographic Characteristics *(Continued)*

Years of operation		
Less than 1 year	33	20.9
1–5 ears	79	50.0
6–10 years	26	16.5
11–15 years	6	3.8
16–20 years	3	1.9
21–25 years	4	2.5
26–30 years	1	0.6
Missing. values	7	3.8
Total	**158**	**100**

Coast entrepreneurial ecosystem, which hosts young female student entrepreneurs from within and outside the university. As a result, more respondents (82.1%) had or were pursuing tertiary education or training, whereas 5.1% had never been to school. Of the remaining respondents, 3.2%, 7.7%, and 1.9% had basic, secondary school, and vocational/technical education, respectively.

Trading was the main business activity (41.1%), followed by service provision (17.2%) and tailoring (11.9%). The less engaged economic activities were cooking and baking (9.2%), farming and aquaculture (7.3%), agro-processing (6.6%) and manufacturing (6.6%). Most respondents (52%) had been in business for one to five years, while 21.7% had less than one year of experience running their businesses. An appreciable number of respondents (17.1%) indicated that they had been in business for 6–10 years. The rest of the respondents had operated their businesses for more than 11–30 years.

Descriptive Statistics

The respondents used numerous digital platforms and services, including Facebook, Tonaton/Jiji, Hubtel, Kikuu, and Jumia. However, the leading digital platforms and services used by the respondents were WhatsApp ($M = 5.92$, SD $= 1.55$) and mobile money services ($M = 5.69$, SD $= 1.56$). Descriptive statistics on the extent to which digitalization empowered the respondents demonstrated mean scores between $M = 4.36$ and 5.92 for all the items that measured psychological, relational, and economic empowerment, which are above the theoretical mean of 4, meaning the extent of influence was high.

Inferential Data Analysis

The dataset was checked for accuracy of data entry and missing values before the quantitative analyses. As a result, we deleted cases with too few or no responses in the variables from the dataset. We used the two-step procedure suggested by Hair et al. (2019) for PLS-SEM analysis (i.e., an assessment of the measurement model and the structural model) to test hypothesized model. The decision to use the PLS-SEM, based on the goal of the study, was to estimate "the model's indicator variables and the structural path without imposing distributional assumptions on the study data" (Hair et al., 2019, p. 2). Also, the PLS-SEM accounts for total variance and uses total variance to estimate parameters as opposed to covariance-based structural equation modeling (CB-SEM) (Hair et al., 2017).

Measurement Model

Before testing the hypothesized relationship, a partial least square was used in performing confirmatory factor analyses (CFA). Specifically, the model tested psychometric properties, including construct reliability, convergent validity, and discriminant validity. This was achieved by way of assessing the model's Cronbach's alpha (α), composite reliability (CR), rho_A, indicator reliability (which was evaluated by considering factor loadings [FL]), average variance extracted (AVE), and discriminant validity. Six digital platforms (Hubtel, Jiji, Tonaton, Kikuu, Jumia, and Twitter) for measuring the digitalization of business operations were deleted due to weak factor loadings and incomplete data. Table 3.2 shows that all the α of the constructs of the variables except those measuring digitalization of business transactions met or exceeded the threshold of 0.70 (Hair et al., 2019).

Furthermore, the values of CR for all the variables (0.747–0.941) met or exceeded the expected threshold (Hair et al., 2019). In terms of the FL, all FL estimates, except for Facebook, Instagram, Momo, and PE5, met the acceptable limit. This indicator was retained because it improved the measurement model's performance, consistent with Hair et al.'s (2019) recommendation. Regarding rho_A, all the estimates, except those for the

Table 3.2   Construct Factor Loading, Reliability, and Convergent Validity

Constructs	Code	FL	CA α	rho_A	CR	AVE
	Fbook	0.638	0.550	0.556	0.747	0.425
Digitalization of business transactions	InstGram	0.601				
	Momo	0.655				
	Wapp	0.710				
	EE1	0.794	0.902	0.922	0.924	0.672
	EE2	0.851				
	EE3	0.902				
Economic Empowerment (EE)	EE4	0.889				
	EE5	0.761				
	EE6	0.705				
	PE1	0.757	0.892	0.902	0.913	0.568
	PE2	0.781				
	PE3	0.778				
Personal and Psychological Empowerment (PE)	PE4	0.783				
	PE5	0.691				
	PE6	0.705				
	PE7	0.773				
	PE8	0.754				
	RE1	0.812	0.921	0.925	0.941	0.761
	RE2	0.915				
	RE3	0.930				
Relational Empowerment (RE)	RE4	0.879				
	RE5	0.821				

digitalization of business, met or exceeded the threshold. We also tested convergent validity by assessing the AVE. In Table 3.2, the AVE for all the variables except those for digitalization of business activities also met or exceeded the threshold indicating no issues with the convergent validity.

Table 3.3   Heterotrait-Monotrait Ratio

	1	2	3	4
1. Digitalization of business transactions				
2. Economic Empowerment	0.462			
3. Psychological Empowerment	0.479	0.786		
4. Relational Empowerment	0.452	0.770	0.799	

Discriminant Validity

The discriminant validity of the model was evaluated by considering the Heterotrait-Monotrait (HTMT). From a conservative threshold, a latent construct has discriminant validity when that HTMT ratio is below 0.850 (Henseler et al., 2015) and the confidence interval, showing the range into which the real HTMT population value will fall, must not possess the value 1 (Hair et al., 2017). In Table 3.3, the estimates related to the HTMT (0.539–0.799) met the tolerable limit. Therefore, based on the results, there were no issues with discriminant validity in the data.

Structural Model

After evaluating the psychometric properties of the model, we assessed the structural model. The structural model was evaluated for the model's predictive accuracy and predictive relevance. This was done by considering R-Square (R^2), Stone-Geisser's Q Square (Q^2) effect size (f^2), and multicollinearity (which was evaluated using the variance inflation factor, VIF) (Hair et al., 2019). Table 3.4 (see Figure 3.2 also) suggests that the digitalization of business transactions predicts (explains) 11.3% of the variance in economic empowerment.

Table 3.4   Structural Model

Constructs	R^2	R^2 adjusted	f^2	Q^2	VIF
Digitalization of business transactions	–	–	–	0.000	–
Economic empowerment	0.113	0.107	0.127	0.072	1.000
Personal and psychological empowerment	0.121	0.116	0.138	0.061	1.000
Relational empowerment	0.108	0.102	0.121	0.079	1.000

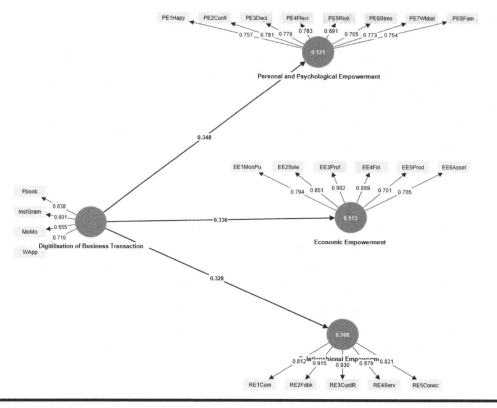

Figure 3.2   Structural path model.

Furthermore, the digitalization of business transactions predicts (explains) 12.1% of the variance in personal and psychological empowerment. Last but not least, the digitalization of business transactions predicts (explains) 10.8% of the variance in relational empowerment.

The f^2 values suggest that the digitalization of business has a small effect on economic empowerment ($f^2 = 0.127$), personal and psychological empowerment ($f^2 = 0.138$), and relational empowerment ($f^2 = 0.121$). Table 3.4 further shows that all the values related to Q^2 were 0 and above, indicating that the model achieved predictive relevance. The model has no multicollinearity problems because the VIF values were less than 3.3, as shown in Table 3.4 (Kock, 2017).

Hypotheses Testing

A bootstrapping procedure with 5,000 re-samples was performed to test the hypothesized relationships. The bootstrapping procedure was further done to confirm whether the study's hypothesized relationships were supported

Table 3.5 Path Coefficient (Direct Effect)

Hyp.	Path	β	T-Statistics	P Values	Supported/ Not supported
H$_1$	DBT -> EE	0.336	5.664	0.000	Supported
H$_2$	DBT -> PE	0.348	6.320	0.000	Supported
H$_3$	DBT -> RE	0.328	5.079	0.000	Supported

Note: DBT = Digitalization of business transactions, EE = economic empowerment, PE = Personal and Psychological Empowerment, RE = Relational Empowerment.

or rejected. Although researchers recommend the control of demographic variables such as age and business size, initial assessment largely resulted in insignificant effects. Table 3.5 shows that the hypothesized relationships (H$_1$–H$_3$) were supported.

Specifically, the results show that the digitalization of business transactions has a significant positive effect on the economic empowerment of female entrepreneurs ($\beta = 0.336$, $t = 5.664$, p-value $= 0.000$). The result could be attributed to an agency in terms of the female entrepreneurs' ability to make and implement strategic entrepreneurial decisions, including investment in digitalizing their operations. Tursunova (2014) and Boateng (2017) underscore the facilitating role of agency in women's empowerment which, in this study, is manifest in the positive influence of the digitalization of business transactions on the economic empowerment of entrepreneurs, in line with prior research by Buer et al. (2021) and Miniesy et al. (2021).

The results further show that the digitalization of business transactions significantly and positively influences the psychological empowerment ($\beta = 0.348$, $t = 6.320$, p-value $= 0.000$) of the female entrepreneurs surveyed. As one of the less researched constructs (Miniesy et al., 2022), this study provides empirical evidence, showing the capacity of digitalization of business operations to promote the psychological empowerment of female entrepreneurs. The findings confirm previous research by Alam et al. (2009) and Ye and Yang (2020).

Finally, the results prove that the digitalization of business transactions positively affects the relational empowerment of female entrepreneurs in a significant manner ($\beta = 0.328$, $t = 5.079$, p-value $= 0.000$). The digital platforms (e.g., WhatsApp and Facebook) that female entrepreneurs use to provide them with the opportunity to communicate and relate with others. This empowers them to give timely information and feedback to clients and other stakeholders. The results are akin to previous studies such as Ye and Yang (2020) and Miniesy et al. (2022). Theoretically, the results support arguments by the liberal feminist theory that when women have access to the requisite resources, they tend to develop the necessary capacity to perform (Foss et al., 2019; Williams & Kedir, 2018).

Conclusion

The purpose of the study was to analyze the effects of digitalization on the empowerment of female entrepreneurs. This study has provided empirical evidence supporting digitalization's positively significant effects on female entrepreneurs' empowerment in the execution of their economic activities. In addition, the study contributes to the emerging research field of digitalization and empowerment by adding to the critically limited number of studies that address female entrepreneurs. The findings suggest that digitalization is an important phenomenon for female entrepreneurship. As a result, female entrepreneurs should undergo orientation of the understanding, usage and effective management of digital platforms and services to have positive returns on their investments.

Limitations and Future Research

Similar to most cross-sectional studies, the data were largely limited to the University of Cape Coast entrepreneurial ecosystem. Data collection was cross-sectional, limiting the ability to assess the causal relationship between the study's constructs. Further, this research does not allow for the generalization of the results due to the sampling technique employed. It is recommended that future studies can focus on longitudinal design and use sampling techniques that allow for generalizations.

Practical and Managerial Implications

This research has shown that digitalization of economic activities positively enhances the empowerment of female entrepreneurs, with the strongest significant influence on their personal and psychological empowerment, followed by their economic empowerment and, last but not least, their relational empowerment. A major implication of this finding is that female entrepreneurs' usage of digital platforms and services in their economic activities is very important to their business operations and personal advancement. The personal and psychological empowerment of female entrepreneurs could have the capacity to augment the effect of digitalization on the relational and economic empowerment of female entrepreneurs to drive the growth and development of their businesses.

Interventions such as digitalization training programs and financial assistance would be critical to support female entrepreneurs in boosting their investments in digital platforms and services. This would enable them to venture into foreign markets for higher returns, business growth and personal, societal, and national development. Digitalization of female entrepreneurs' economic activities, thus, becomes fundamental to the attainment of the SDGs, particularly goal 1 on ending poverty; goal 5, which focuses on gender equality and empowering women and girls; and goal 8, which touches on decent work and economic growth.

References

Afshar, H. (Ed.) (1998). *Women and Empowermrnt: Illustion from the Third World* (First ed.). New York, USA: St. Martin's Press, Inc.

Ahl, H., & Marlow, S. (2012). Exploring the dynamics of gender, feminism and entrepreneurship: Advancing debate to escape a dead end? *Organization, 19*(5), 543–562. https://doi.org/10.1177/1350508412448695

Alam, Q., Yusuf, M. A., & Coghill, K. (2009). Village phone program, commodification of mobile phone set and empowerment of women. *Journal of Community Informatics, 5*(3–4) [Online].

Al Dahdah, M. (2021). From Ghana to India, saving the Global South's mothers with a digital solution. *Global Policy, 12*, 45–54. https://doi.org/10.1111/1758-5899.12939

Ali, J., & Shabir, S. (2017). Does gender make a difference in business performance? Evidence from a large enterprise survey data of India. *Gender in Management: An International Journal, 32*(3): 218–233. https://doi.org/10.1108/GM-09-2016-0159

Alkhaled, S., & Berglund, K. (2018). 'And now I'm free': Women's empowerment and emancipation through entrepreneurship in Saudi Arabia and Sweden. *Entrepreneurship & Regional Development, 30*(7–8), 877–900. https://doi.org/10.1080/08985626.2018.1500645

Banda, F. (2006). Women, law and human rights in Southern Africa. *Journal of Southern African Studies, 32*(1), 13–27. https://doi.org/10.1080/03057070500493720

Batliwala, S. (1994) The meaning of Women's empowerment: New concepts from Action. In G. Sen, A. Germain and L. C. Chen (eds.), *Population Policies Reconsidered. Health, Empowerment and Rights* (pp. 127–138). Cambridge, MA: Harvard University Press.

Bhutani, S., & Paliwal, Y. (2015). Digitalization: A step towards sustainable development. *OIDA International Journal of Sustainable Development,* *8*(12), 11–24. Retrieved from http://www.ssrn.com/link/OIDA-Intl-Journal-Sustainable-Dev.html

Boateng, J. S. (2017). *Women in District Assemblies in Ghana: Gender construction, resistance, and empowerment.* Doctoral Thesis Submited to Edith Cowan University. Joondalup Australia: Edith Cowan University. Retrieved from http://ro.ecu.edu.au/theses/2048

Boateng, J. S., Banham, V., Kosi, I., & Ayentimi, D. T. (2021). Socialization and women's participation in governance: Exploring important themes from Ghana'. *International Journal of Gender Studies in Developing Societies, 4*(1), 75–94. Retrieved from https://www.inderscienceonline.com/doi/abs/10.1504/IJGSDS.2021.112142

Boohene, R. (2009). The relationships among gender, strategic capabilities, and performance of small retail firms in Ghana. *Journal of African Business, 10*(1), 121–138. https://doi.org/10.1080/15228910802701601

Briggs, J. (2022). *Digital Empowerment and Role of Culture in Digital Transformation.* Retrieved from https://www.ionology.com/digital-empowerment/

Budgeon, S. (2015). Individualized femininity and feminist politics of choice. *European Journal of Women's Studies, 22*(3), 303–318. https://doi.org/10.1177/1350506815576602

Buer, S. V., Semini, M., Strandhagen, J. O., & Sgarbossa, F. (2021). The complementary effect of lean manufacturing and digitalization on operational performance. *International Journal of Production Research, 59*(7), 1976–1992. https://doi.org/10.1080/00207543.2020.1790684

Chakraborty, A. (2019). Digital India campaign and Indian women: A critical study. *International Journal of Research and Analytical Reviews, 6*(2), 249–251. https://doi.org/10.1163/9789004432284_056

Creswell, J. W., & Creswell, J. D. (2018). *Research Design. Qualitative, Quantitative and Mixed Methods Approaches* (5th ed.). London: SAGE Publications, Inc.

Dejene, Y. (2007), Promoting women's economic empowerment in Africa. Africa Economic Conference, Addis Ababa, November, pp. 15–17.

van Dop, N., Depauw, J., & Driessens, K. (2016). Measuring empowerment: Development and validation of the service user psychological empowerment scale. *Journal of Social Service Research, 42*(5), 651–664. https://doi.org/10.1080/01488376.2016.1216915

Elam, A. B., Hughes, K. D., Guerrero, M., Hill, S., & Nawangpalupi, C. (2021). *Women's Entrepreneurship 2020/21. Thriving Through Crisis.* London, UK: Global Entrepreneurship Research Association, London Business School.

Foss, L., Henry, C., Ahl, H., & Mikalsen, G. H. (2019). Women's entrepreneurship policy research: A 30-year review of the evidence. *Small Business Economics, 53*(2), 409–429. https://doi.org/10.1007/s11187-018-9993-8

Hair, J., Hollingsworth, C. L., Randolph, A. B., & Chong, A. Y. L. (2017). An updated and expanded assessment of PLS-SEM in information systems research.

Industrial Management & Data Systems, 117(3), 442–458. https://doi.org/10.1108/IMDS-04-2016-0130

Hair, J. F., Risher, J. J., Sarstedt, M., & Ringle, C. M. (2019). When to use and how to report the results of PLS-SEM. *European Business Review, 31*(1), 2–24. https://doi.org/10.1108/EBR-11-2018-0203

Hekman, S. (1997). Reply to Hartsock, Collins, Harding, and Smith. *Signs: Journal of Women in Culture and Society, 22*(2), 399–402. Retrieved from https://www.journals.uchicago.edu/doi/pdf/10.1086/495159?casa_token

Henseler, J., Ringle, C. M., & Sarstedt, M. (2015). A new criterion for assessing discriminant validity in variance-based structural equation modeling. *Journal of the Academy of Marketing Science, 43*, 115–135.

Huang, G. Q., Zhao, J. B., & Chen, X. (2007). "Do It Yourself (DIY) Portalets" for developing e-business solutions for small and medium enterprises. *Journal of Manufacturing Technology Management, 18*, 72–89.

Ihalainen, M., Schure, J., & Sola, P. (2020). Where are the women? A review and conceptual framework for addressing gender equity in charcoal value chains in Sub-Saharan Africa. *Energy for Sustainable Development, 55*, 1–12. https://doi.org/10.1016/j.esd.2019.11.003

Kabeer, N. (1999). *The Conditions and Consequences of Choice: Reflections on the Measurement of women's Empowerment* (Vol. 108, pp. 1–58). Geneva: UNRISD.

Kabeer, N. (2001). Reflections on the measurement of Women's empowerment—Theory and practice. In A. Sisask (Ed.), Discussing Women's Empowerment—Theory and Practice (pp. 17–54). Stockholm, Sweden: Novum Grafiska AB.

Kabeer, N. (2020). Women's empowerment and economic development: A feminist critique of storytelling practices in "randomista" economics. *Feminist Economics, 26*(2), 1–26.

Keller, B., & Mbewe, D. C. (1991). Policy and planning for the empowerment of Zambia's women farmers. *Canadian Journal of Development Studies/Revue canadienne d'études du développement, 12*(1), 75–88.

Kock, N. (2017). *WarpPLS user manual: Version 6.0.* ScriptWarp Systems: Laredo, TX, USA, 141.

Kogiso, M., Yu, L., Masuda, R., Gupta, G., Koyama, N., Oberoi, J. V., & Reddy, S. (2017). *Advancing women's Empowerment: ICT Skills for Girls and Women in Southeast Asia.* The Sasakawa Peace Foundation and Dalberg Global Development Advisors, Tokyo, Japan.

Kontos, E., Blake, K. D., Chou, W. Y. S., & Prestin, A. (2014). Predictors of eHealth usage: Insights on the digital divide from the Health Information National Trends Survey 2012. *Journal of Medical Internet Research, 16*(7), e3117.

Kurtiş, T., Adams, G., & Estrada-Villalta, S. (2016). Decolonizing empowerment: Implications for sustainable well-being. *Analyses of Social Issues and Public Policy, 16*(1), 387–391.

Kuusisto, M. (2017). Organizational effects of digitalization: A literature review. *International Journal of Organization Theory and Behavior, 20*(03), 341–362.

Lal, T. (2021). Impact of financial inclusion on economic development of marginalized communities through the mediation of social and economic empowerment. *International Journal of Social Economics, 48*(12), 1768–1793.

Marlow, S. (2020). Gender and entrepreneurship: Past achievements and future possibilities. *International Journal of Gender and Entrepreneurship, 12*(1), 39–52.

Maxwell, H., O'Shea, M., Stronach, M., & Pearce, S. (2021). Empowerment through digital health trackers: An exploration of Indigenous Australian women and physical activity in leisure settings. *Annals of Leisure Research, 24*(1), 150–167. https://doi.org/10.1080/11745398.2019.1674677

McKeown, N., & Durkin, M. (2017). *The Seven Principles of Digital Business Strategy*. New York, NY: Business Expert Press..

Miniesy, R., Elshahawy, E., & Fakhreldin, H. (2022). Social media's impact on the empowerment of women and youth male entrepreneurs in Egypt. *International Journal of Gender and Entrepreneurship, 14*(2), 235–252. https://doi.org/10.1108/IJGE-06-2021-0085

Miniesy, R., Shahin, M., & Fakhreldin, H. (2021, September). *Factors Behind Digital Entrepreneurship Adoption by Egyptian MSEs*. In European Conference on Innovation and Entrepreneurship (pp. 573–582). Reading, UK: Academic Conferences International Limited.

Penney, E. K., Agyei, J., Boadi, E. K., Abrokwah, E., & Ofori-Boafo, R. (2021). Understanding factors that influence consumer intention to use mobile money services: An application of UTAUT2 with perceived risk and trust. *SAGE Open, 11*(3), 1–17. https://doi.org/10.1177/21582440211023188

Prasad, D. R. (2014). Women Empowerment in Urban Governance in India. Indian Journal of Public Administration, *60*(3), 426–442. https://doi.org/10.1177/0019556120140305

Schillo, R. S., & Ebrahimi, H. (2022). Gender dimensions of digitalization: A comparison of Venture Capital backed start-ups across fields. *Technology Analysis & Strategic Management, 34*(7), 733–745. https://doi.org/10.1080/09537325.2021.1918336

Sen, G. (1994). Women's empowerment and human rights: the challenge to policy. In: Graham-Smith F, (ed). A report of the population summit of the World's scientific academy. London: Royal Society London.

Shen, H., Fu, M., Pan, H., Yu, Z., & Chen, Y. (2020). The impact of the COVID-19 pandemic on firm performance. *Emerging Markets Finance and Trade, 56*(10), 2213–2230. https://doi.org/10.1080/1540496X.2020.1785863

Tech Target. (2022). *Definition: Digitisation*. Retrieved from https://www.techtarget.com/whatis/definition/digitization

Tsan, M., Totapally, S., Hailu, M., & Addom, B. K. (2019). *The Digitalisation of African Agriculture Report 2018–2019*. Wageningen, The Netherlands: CTA/Dalberg Advisers.

Tursunova, Z. (2014). Women's Narratives: Resistance to Oppression and the Empowerment of Women in Uzbekistan. *Journal of Indigenous Social Development, 3*(2), 1–16.

United Nations Development Program [UNDP]. (2015). The Millennium Development Goals Report 2015. Retrieved from https://www.un.org/millenniumgoals/2015_MDG_Report/pdf/MDG%202015%20rev%20(July%201).pdf

Williams, C. C., & Kedir, A. (2018). Contesting the underperformance thesis of women entrepreneurs: Firm-level evidence from South Africa. *International Journal of Management and Enterprise Development, 17*(1), 21–35. https://doi.org/10.1504/IJMED.2018.088327

Ye, L., & Yang, H. (2020). From digital divide to social inclusion: A tale of mobile platform empowerment in rural areas. *Sustainability, 12*(6), 2424. https://doi.org/10.3390/su12062424

Yu, F., Jiang, D., Zhang, Y., & Du, H. (2021). Enterprise digitalization and financial performance: The moderating role of dynamic capability. *Technology Analysis & Strategic Management*, 1–17. https://doi.org/10.1080/09537325.2021.1980211

Appendix

Table A3.1 Digitalization Scale

		Less often		Very often						
	Digital platforms & services	NO	YES	1	2	3	4	5	6	7
1.	Mobile money services									
2.	WhatsApp									
3.	Facebook									
4.	Instagram									
5.	Twitter									
6.	Jumia									
7.	Kikuu									
8.	Tonaton									
9.	Jiji									
10.	Hubtel									
	In the spaces below, please specify *other platforms that you use* and rate									
11.										
12.										
13.										

Table A3.2 Female Empowerment Scale

	Least extent	High extent						
		1	2	3	4	5	6	7
	Psychological empowerment: **Through the use of the digital platforms & services, I ...**							
1.	am happy about the performance of my business							
2.	am confident about my ability to grow the business							
3.	am able to make better decisions about my business							
4.	have developed the flexibility in the use of the platform(s)							
5.	am able to manage risk in digital fraud							
6.	am able to manage stress							
7.	am able to balance work and family							
8.	have improved the well-being of my family							
	Relational empowerment: **Through the use of the digital platforms & services, I ...**							
1.	communicate often with my customers and others							
2.	give quick feedback to customers, etc.							
3.	have been able to improve my relationship with my customers, suppliers, etc.							
4.	serve my customers better							
5.	connect with new customers quicker							
6.	teach others on the use of the platform							
	Economic empowerment: **Through the use of the digital platforms & services, ...**							
1.	I am able to monitor my purchases better							
2.	I have increased my monthly sales							
3.	My profits have increased							
4.	My financial condition has improved							
5.	I have been able to add more products to my business							
6.	I have been able to acquire other business assets							

Chapter 4

Entertaining Development from Downstream: Village-Owned Enterprises, Women's Empowerment, and Information Technology in Binor Probolinggo Village and Pujon Kidul Village, Indonesia

M. Zaenul Muttaqin and Made Selly Dwi Suryanti
Cenderawasih University, Waena Street, Jayapura City 99224, Indonesia

Rohim Rohim
STIA Pembangunan, Lumba-Lumba Street, Jember Regency 68122, Indonesia

Contents

DOI: 10.4324/9781003302346-4

Introduction

The basic assumption of the people-centered development paradigm is that human resources are the primary determinant of development success. This assumption rests on the fact that several countries with high-quality human resources have achieved economic growth despite being poor in natural resources within two to three decades. Human resources have a central position in realizing development performance.

In Indonesia, we can trace the people-centered development within village-owned enterprises (BUMDes) as grassroots social institutions. The BUMDes institution is a rural-based social institution that provides social services. According to Ilham et al. (2020), the main objectives of establishing BUMDes are to improve the rural economy, support the village's original income, develop asset management according to the needs of the village community, and centralize the villages as the backbone of equitable economic development. The development of BUMDes refers to the policy products of Village Law no. 6/2014 concerning Villages. This law contains recognition and legal status at the village-level government system, supporting village community tradition and culture systems, supporting increased village community participation in the government system accelerated services based on village independence (Wahab et al., 2022).

Kafabih (2018) explains that to achieve development goals as contained in the Village Law, the government is following up on a funding scheme through Government Regulation no. 60/2014 concerning Village Funds. With this capital scheme, the village government can find the community's service needs and support them to participate in development. In essence, the story of BUMDes is synonymous with economic motives that support village economic development based on autonomous government resources and village communities (Bagus, 2020; Nursetiawan, 2018).

In contemporary developments, BUMDes development faces several obstacles. These barriers generally include organizational management and the competence of managers within it. Previous studies have shown that the challenges in managing BUMDes revolve around the weak synergize among business actors in rural areas and BUMDes, vulnerable marketing networks, and a lack of facilities and infrastructure (Nursan & Utama-FR, 2019; Siagan, 2021; Sulaksana & Nuryanti, 2019; Wahab et al., 2022). With these various weaknesses, the main objective of BUMDes requires several supporting factors other than mere capital, such as the development of training and outreach, which directly contribute to increasing the capacity of human resources and institutional asset management.

However, most of the previous studies have not reviewed the involvement of women in the development of BUMDes. Similar studies analyze BUMDes development in general without placing frictions and highlighting gender stratification in the rural development paradigm. This study further explores the critical role of women in BUMDes to complement the previous study. In addition, this study aims to explore village women's empowerment programs and study stakeholder involvement through small businesses that synergize with BUMDes. The central assumption is to highlight women's empowerment through BUMDes in an optimistic way. Preliminary study studies show that two BUMDes provide opportunities for women's participation in their management; Binor Energy BUMDes in Binor Probolinggo Village and Sumber Sejahtera BUMDes in Pujon Kidul Village, Malang Regency. Even though they are in two different locations, the two BUMDes develop aligned innovations. First, creation by developing the village's potential to become a tourist village can also support the development of micro, small, and medium enterprises (MSMEs). Second, in the management of BUMDes, the two towns prioritize the role of women as the key to success—third, the use of digital technology as an instrument for promoting tourism villages.

Concept Explanation

The Development

Development is a process of planned change involving a cycle of life improvement (Haryati et al., 2020). It includes improving the quality of all human lives (Ismail, 2020). In this sense, development consists of three equally important aspects, enhancing the life of the nation, creating conditions that can foster a sense of self-esteem, and developing the freedom to choose by expanding opportunities.

The outlined development to achieve the goals, five development strategies underlie the process of implementing development in a country, namely the welfare state, neo-economic, structuralist, and humanizing. However, according to Sulistyastuti (2004), of the five strategies, only two have been widely implemented. The first is growth which emphasizes the trickle-down effect and growth theory. The concept of Development embraced by millions of people in the Third World reflects the western paradigm of social change development with step-by-step movement toward higher modernity. Industrialized countries achieve modernity that reflects technological, economic development and progress.

The future strategy is welfare state to emphasize redistribution growth. Adelman and Morris (1973) once argued that in the first stages, basic policies that only prioritize increasing the rate of development or production often do not support social justice for small communities. Because, in the first stage, the 5% of the highest structure in society will get multiple benefits. Meanwhile, the small group, which is 40% below, obtains a low level of social welfare. The top 20%, on average, receive all income. Adelman and Morris (1973) consider that the essence of development is significant social changes. Therefore, it must be gradual to avoid accesses that can harm the development process.

Gender

Social scientists introduce the concept of gender to explain the difference between men and women as part of something that is "given" and as part of a culture and the result of the construction of society. This distinction is important because there is often a mixture of natural and non-natural (gender) human characteristics. This difference in gender roles helps us rethink the division of roles. It so far has been considered to be inherent in women and men to create a description of gender relations that is dynamic and appropriate to the realities in society.

The concept of gender has produced several differences in terms of roles, responsibilities, functions, and even the space in which humans move. The word of gender has differences in roles, status, operations, and commitments to men and women due to sociocultural constructions that have taken root through socialization from one generation to the next. Therefore, gender is dynamic and can be exchanged from one human to another depending on the culture in each region.

Referring to Puspitawati (2013), gender can be defined as follows; gender refers to the economic, social, politic, and culture attributes, and opportunities associated with being male and female. The social definition of what it meant to be a woman or man varies among cultures and changes over time, conceptualizing gender as a set of relations; it exists in social institutions, and interpersonal interaction reproduces it (Lloyd, 2007). Gender theory is a social constructionist perspective that simultaneously examines the ideological and the material levels of analyzes (Lloyd, 2007).

From these two explanations, gender is a term that carries social rules related to human sexuality. Gender is different from sex, which is a term related to human biology and both men and women have reproductive organs. However, gender interprets as the result of human ideas and assigns roles to women and men.

Efforts to empower women in Indonesia in development are an integral and inseparable part of national development. Women's empowerment in various fields of life reflects the equality of rights, obligations, roles, and opportunities between the two per the philosophy and culture of the nation endeavored to always lead to the realization of equality with gender justice. Gender equality is a dynamic condition in which men and women both have rights, obligations, roles, and opportunities based on mutual respect and appreciation, as well as assistance in various sectors.

The women empowerment in BUMDes supports the expansion of women's activities which focused on the domestic sphere toward the non-domestic. With the existence of BUMDes, activities previously for primary domestic needs have shifted to non-domestic activities to support the family economy. In short, BUMDes has opened employment opportunities for skilled women in rural areas.

Concerning BUMDes, the author examines that the role of women has not been visible. However, what must be known is that, in managing BUMDes, the role of the women behind it has considerable influence in managing Sumber Sejahtera BUMDes. It is essential to look at it from the side of equality and equity to realize that men and women both have the same role in access, participation, control, and benefits.

Digital Economy

The concept of the digital economy has been developing for a long time since Information and Communications Technology (ICT) existed and has been used globally. The world economy has gone through four stages, starting from the agricultural society stage, the machine era after the industrial revolution, the oil hunt era, and the era of multinational corporate capitalism (Olsson and Hibbs Jr., 2005). Only certain elite groups with owners of capital are able to have these four waves.

With the development of ICT, then comes the digital economy with more significant opportunities. Because the previous economic development only brought benefits that certain groups could utilize. The concept of the digital economy has a competitive character, which has given the industry a new spirit. It because easily picked up by startups who prioritize the importance of synergize and collaboration in the industry. Therefore, the e-digital economy can be said to be a form of sharing economy that elevates many MSMEs to enter the technology-based business world.

In the economy, there are various potential sectors, namely: first, the financial industry, characterized by the emergence of various digital applications as a means of payment, proves that the rupiah shows the development of the digital economy. In Indonesia, fintech or financial technology has begun to be developed and introduced by digital economy business players. Indonesian government oversees the development of fintech in its operation, namely the Financial Services Authority and Bank Indonesia. In the fintech industry, the payment system developed as a non-cash payment tool, i.e., the OVO, Go-Pay, Dana, and LinkAja applications. Second, the funding system is usually finteched in the lending sector in Indonesia. The third is on other fintech systems, namely on fintech platform organizers outside the payment and funding system.

Then in other fintech fields, you can find it in digital banking, such as kitabisa.com, Jenius by BTPN, and Digibank by DBS. Second, Culture, Tourism, and Creative Economy Sectors. In this sector, readers can see that in promoting tourism, tourism actors use e-commerce platforms to promote cultural products, local people's creativity, and natural tourism potential. Usually, the applications readers can find are Traveloka,

Pegi-Pegi, and Tiket.com. These three things are examples of innovation and development through the digital economy. Three agricultural sectors in this sector it is predicted that there will be changes due to the adaptation of robotic technology and the Internet of Things (IoT) which can bring the agricultural sector toward agriculture 4.0 if technology 4.0 is implemented, of course, this will get various kinds of changes to both the producers and consumers. One of them is that consumers will be closer to farmers because the transaction process for agricultural products is faster and more effective. Apart from being in the transaction process, it opens up opportunities to strengthen productivity. The value of more comprehensive agricultural businesses such as agriculture, animal husbandry, fisheries, and forestry will increase. Sample text—Every country needs to act immediately to prepare, respond, and recover. United Nations Secretary-General António Guterres has launched a US$2 billion global humanitarian response plan in the most vulnerable. Developing countries could lose at least US$220 billion in income, and the United Nations Conference on Trade and Development has called for US$2.5 trillion to support them.

Drawing on our experience with other outbreaks such as Ebola, HIV, SARS, TB, and malaria, as well as our long history of working with the private and public sector, UNDP will help countries to urgently and effectively respond to COVID-19 as part of its mission to eradicate poverty, reduce inequalities and build resilience to crises and shocks.

Study Methods

The study paradigm used in this study is a qualitative study with a descriptive study type. The purpose of this descriptive study is to describe in the form of descriptive words and not numbers so that what is collected becomes the key to what has been studied (Moleong, 2016). Determination of informants in this study use purposive sampling. The collected data was conducted by interviewing key informants, namely the director of Bumdes Bhinor Energi (Probolinggo Regency), namely Mr. Abdul Komar and Mr. Udi Hartoko as the director of Bumdes Sumber Sejahtera (Malang Regency). Meanwhile, additional informants selected purposively have affected residents from the Bumdes business unit. Meanwhile, secondary data from field observations during fieldwork. Data analyzes went through the stages of reduction, description, explanation, and interpretation.

Study Context

Law of the Republic of Indonesia Number 6 of 2014 concerning Villages has tremendous implications for village development. The law is based on the principle of recognition and the direction of subsidiarity which allows the village to become the subject and actor of the story, no longer an object of the action. The Village Law gives sovereignty and authority to villages to regulate themselves either through origin authority, local village scale authority, or assignment. Thus, the town becomes the smallest administrative unit which is the spearhead of Indonesia's development. "Village builds and builds villages" is the slogan and noble aspiration to build Indonesia from the village.

Based on data published by the Ministry of Villages, Development of Disadvantaged Regions, and Transmigration (Kemendes PDTT) launched, the Developing Village Index (IDM), a national IDM calculation covering 73,709 villages throughout Indonesia.

The status of village independence and progress is a parameter for adjusting budget interventions in development policies. Based on Table 4.1, from 2019 to 2022, there has been a significant increase in village status. Villages in the criteria for being independent in 840 will experience an increase in 2020, with a total of 1,741 separate villages with a percentage of 2.49%. Then the requirements for an independent town will increase in 2021 with a total of 3,278 villages and double in 2022 with a total of 6,239 separate villages or around 8.44%.

Table 4.1 Developing Village Index (IDM)

Criteria	2019	2020	2021	2022
Independent	840 (1.22%)	1,741 (2.49%)	3,278 (4.44%)	6,239 (8.44%)
Advanced	8,647 (12.56%)	11,899 (17.01%)	15,324 (20.75%)	20,247 (27.38%)
Developing	38,185 (55.47%)	39,866 (57.01%)	38,086 (51.57%)	33,881 (45.81%)
Fairy underdeveloped	17,626 (25.61%)	13,961 (19.96%)	12,177 (16.49%)	9,220 (12.47%)
Underdeveloped	3,536 (5.14%)	2,466 (3.53%)	4,985 (6.75%)	4,366 (5.90%)

Source: Ministry of Village (2022).

The Developing Village Index (IDM) is a composite index formed based on social, economic, and environmental resilience indices that is released by the Ministry of Villages.

In a strategic effort to build from villages, the Ministry of Villages PDTT designed a unique work program in the Nawacita Prioritas for the 2015–2019 period, including: (1) preparing the implementation of village fund distribution of IDR 1.4 billion per village in stages and (2) preparing and developing 5,000 BUMDes (Village Owned Enterprises) (Nurpuspita et al., 2019). This effort has shown remarkable results; for the five years of the National Medium Term Development Plan (RPJMN 2014–2019), 2014 1,022 BUMDes exceeded the target of 5,000 BUMDes, becoming 45,549 BUMDes at the end of 2018 (Nasrulhaq, 2019).

BUMDes existed before the issuance of the Village Law. However, its existence has become increasingly strategic because of its essential role as a supporter of village economic resilience. The mandate to establish BUMDes as a supporter of village economic resilience has been rolled out and regulated in various laws and regulations, such as Regulation of the Minister of Villages, Development of Disadvantaged Regions, and Transmigration of the Republic of Indonesia No. 4 of 2015 concerning Establishment, Management and Management, and Dissolution of Village-Owned Enterprises and Ministerial Regulations Villages, Development of Disadvantaged Regions, and Transmigration of the Republic of Indonesia No. 22 of 2016 concerning Setting Priorities for the Use of Village Funds for 2017. Even though various regulations as an umbrella for establishing BUMDes, and the achievement of many BUMDes that has exceeded the target, most BUMDes are still not yet operational.

In its development, by facilitating the growth of MSMEs, stretch BUMDes management. MSMEs are productive business units that stand alone, and individuals or business entities carry all economic sectors. MSMEs are effective businesses to support macro and micro-economic development in Indonesia and influence other sectors to build (Suci, 2017). MSMEs have a vast number and potential to absorb labor, so their contribution to the formation of gross domestic product (GDP) is also quite enormous. MSMEs can provide opportunities for micro and small economic actors in society. It can work profitably for the community and BUMDes because they can collaborate in developing businesses owned by the community and business units owned by BUMDes. The existence of micro-enterprises largely determines village economic development. On the other hand, BUMDes can move as long as they get support from the community to participate in aligning the goals of their formation so that BUMDes and community micro-enterprises are in symbiosis with each other to support village development.

The study is in two villages that empower women in the management of BUMDes. The two villages take advantage of the marine and agricultural potential to become tourist areas. Minor Village is in the Paiton District, Probolinggo Regency, one of 325 villages in the Probolinggo region that have succeeded in developing a marine tourism village. With the initiation of the village head, BUMDes in this village have an essential role in managing existing potential by involving the role and participation of women. Meanwhile, BUMDes Sumber Sejahtera, Pujon Kidul Village, Malang Regency, develops agricultural and livestock-based business units (Utami et al., 2022). Women in this BUMDes play an active role in developing business units, especially businesses created by women, to support increasing the village's original income.

Results and Discussion

The development of a tourist village as a community empowerment program provides power and reduces poverty in an area by cultivating local potential in the area (Mustangin et al., 2017). Through tourism villages, the community will benefit from many tourists who enter and the practical benefits for improving people's lives. It is in line with the Regulation of the Minister of Tourism of the Republic of Indonesia No. 13/2018 concerning the Strategic Plan of the Ministry of Tourism for 2018–2019, namely the development of rural-based tourism (tourism villages) will drive tourism economic activities in rural areas which will prevent the urbanization of rural communities to cities. The story of rural tourism will encourage the preservation of nature (among other things: landscapes, rice fields, rivers, and lakes), which in turn will have an impact on reducing global warming. The tourism village program makes a positive contribution to community development.

BUMDes Binor Energi

In 2020, Binor Energi BUMDes won a prestigious award, namely Second Place in the BUMDes Competition held by the Village Community Empowerment Service Office of East Java Province and First Place in the Community Development and Engagement category at the BUMDes Award 2020 event by Ten November Institute of Technology (ITS) Surabaya (Probolinggo Regency Government, 2020). Getting this award requires hard work involving multiple parties, with the critical role being the village government and village internal institutions. A strong BUMDes have to be accompanied by activities involving other parties to develop BUMDes produces an effective formula so that BUMDes succeeds in achieving its goals.

BUMDes Initiation as a Forum for Women's Empowerment

Binor BUMDes management is a form of taking the role of the village head as a women leader who sees village potential that can be independently managed by the village to increase village income (Rohim et al., 2021), as the Village Head and initiator of improving the management of tourist attractions, shows that the beach in Binor Village has various potentials. The beach has good potential for economic activities because it has good coral and has used for tourism activities such as snorkeling. Every year a formal event is held, namely, pick the sea, by providing opportunities for cultural tourism-based tourism. The traditional value of selecting the sea links with the social life of the community around the coast actualizes gratitude for the source of income from the sea. For fishermen, the wealth of marine resources in Binor Village is an integral part of the community's livelihood to build a family economy. The objectives of establishing BUMDes and designing village economic empowerment programs can align these components.

The majority of the Binor village community work as fishermen, which is one of the pillars for the village government to facilitate the development of employment opportunities other than fishing. Then so far, women have had a business (making products) such as packaged stick products, such as mustard sticks, celery, corn, red spinach, spinach, and golden branches. These small businesses need to be accommodated in various ways including the development of tourism objects. Before BUMDes existed, people sold their products independently or individually at their homes. Based on these facts, BUMDes Binor Energi cooperates with Citra Lestari UMKM to empower the community by providing product manufacturing training and helping market products produced by the community to be sold online through social media or deposited at BUMDes both on the west and east coasts.

In addition to processed products, MSMEs help fishing communities by buying catches from the sea. The fishing community feels an extraordinary impact because fish is caught from the ocean which does not need to be sold outside the area as before. BUMDes, in this case, apart from being engaged in tourism, villages are also involved in the culinary business. BUMDes facilitates the marketing and promotion of community businesses outside the region so that people who own businesses do not face too many difficulties in marketing. Based on the results of an interview with the Head of BUMDes, Mr. Abdul Komar explained that the culinary business is the business unit that gets the most profits compared to the tourism business unit. It shows that the impact of tourist objects affects companies around the tourist attraction area. The community's economy also developed and helped meet family needs since the government introduced the tourism village business. First, the facts show that many people are interested in pursuing a culinary business— the potential for increased visits and the comfortable management of tourist objects as the base. With a strategic location with cross-provincial roads, Binor Village has an excellent opportunity to be visited by tourists from other regions to buy culinary products and businesses. Thus, tourists who want to tour Banyuwangi, Bali, or drop by at BUMDes Binor Energi because the seafood culinary business unit managed by BUMDes has a different taste from culinary seafood businesses elsewhere. BUMDes managers can apply this strategic geography to promote their culinary business.

BUMDes cooperates with local MSMEs and provides them facilities so that there is a substantial institutional synergize to lift the village economy, including community welfare. One of the MSMEs that collaborates with BUMDes Binor Energi is Citra Lestari UMKM. This MSME focuses on the culinary business of catching fish. With good cooperation, MSME turnover has increased significantly, meaning that this BUMDes collaboration has a positive impact because it can move the wheels of the community's economy.

Steps to restore the condition of the beach environment over time increased the number of visits to Binor beach. The village government then accommodated this potential by building the Dewi Harmoni Market. The concept of this market is relatively simple, held once a week on every weekend, and aims to mediate the community's economic needs with beach visitors.

However, the whole program is not only to accommodate the existing potential. The Village Government optimizes the participation of women from the Family Welfare Empowerment Team (TPPKK) as a form of support in improving human resource development programs. This non-formal organization is a form of communication between women. At each meeting, the TPPKK routinely discussed how to optimize the potential that existed in the village, which in turn affirmed the formation of BUMDes Binor Energi.

In 2018, the central government established the BUMDes with an investment of IDR 75 million. This capital is for making paving, gazebos, and stalls for villagers to sell local products. Over time, in 2019, building a new business unit on the east coast is a step forward for BUMDes Binor Energi. The east side of the beach is called Bohay Beach; the culinary and tourism industry and selling local community products engage the new BUMDes business on this beach. It is in line with the opinion of Mustangin et al. (2017), who explains that BUMDes development relies on the roles of women in it. These women have the potential to make an essential contribution to BUMDes development as well as local-based economic development.

BUMDes Promotion through Social Media

In marketing promotions, Binor Energi BUMDes and Sumber Sejahtera BUMDes utilize social media and websites as the main tools. These social media include Instagram, Facebook, Instagram, and YouTube. Initially, information technology was considered inadequate for marketing BUMDes products. Most women use conventional methods. However, along the journey, women began to realize and use social media as part of BUMDes' marketing strategy after seeing how fast and efficient the circulation of information on social media was. How BUMDes encourages its employees to post the latest information about tourist attractions in Binor village through their social media accounts and form a special team that operates social media shows the seriousness of BUMDes managers in using social media as a domain. It is in line with Maulana et al.'s study (2022), which explains that this particular team operationalizes social media as a channel for tourism promotion, events, and marketing of business unit products under BUMDes.

BUMDes Sumber Sejahtera

BUMDes, founded in 2015, initially managed the sources of funds disbursed by the central government through village funds. Most budget priorities have been devoted to community empowerment since the BUMDes found. The management of BUMDes is considered as part of women's resources in operating the business units. Women in the Sumber Sejahtera BUMDes organizational structure occupies strategic positions as chairman and treasurer with a high school and undergraduate educational background (Rohim et al., 2021). There are several considerations for women with adequate education in the BUMDes structure. First, women are assumed to have skills in managing business and financial units. Second, women have foresight in the field of administration compared to men. Third, orderly administration must be considered because BUMDes must be able to present transparent and accountable financial reports. The report impacts the level of trust of BUMDes members and interested parties in BUMDes management. Sonowal (2013) in his study stated that women's education influences women's practical experience in their work. Education has an impact on efforts to build the economy. These aspects form the basis for considering the inclusion of women in the organizational structure.

Involvement of Women in the BUMDes Institution

In its management, BUMDes includes potential women as part of human resources in operating the business units they own. There are two reasons for women to become strategic partners of BUMDes. First, women's networks are more open. Village women have specific forums that are permanent. This forum resolves many social-related issues.

On the other hand, this forum is open regarding technical activities and financial management. Usually, these women join forums such as the PKK, a platform for women with families. Meanwhile, women who are young and not yet married have meetings according to their interests and talents.

Second, so far, the village's potential is closer to women. The potential sources of the town are attached to women's daily lives. Geographically, Pujon Kidul Village is agricultural and livestock land. Women are trusted as agents for empowering economic resources in the village. So that BUMDes can have professional governance. In general, women have higher discipline than men. Different interpretations of reality make women use instinct more than men, who seem rigid and fixated on the rationality of rules (Hamidullah et al., 2015). Falk and Hermle (2018) explained that women's empathy for other people is more dominant than men, both in the social context and in work dynamics.

The absorption of women in the Sumber Sejahtera BUMDes in Pujon District includes 30 people in the production of typical batik crafts, the KRPL Women Farmer Group (Sustainable Food Friendly Families) with 15 members in the production of processed agricultural food products. Meanwhile, in the health sector, BUMDes uses the remaining business results (SHU) for the distribution of additional nutrition in the Integrated Service Post (Posyandu), which involves Family Welfare Empowerment (PKK) with 80 women members.

Nursan and Utama-FR (2019), in their study, shows that polishing the theme that BUMDes depends on the potential they have, including the agricultural sector. The development of BUMDes indirectly opens up space for gender-based division of labor. The classification of women's and men's work in the observations at Pujon Village agriculture shows that men tend to work in cultivating agricultural production. Meanwhile, women work in marketing agricultural business products, especially food ingredients, in line with the findings of Termine and Percic's (2015) study, which showed that the mobility of men tends to be greater than that of women because men are more skilled in agricultural work. Based on data from the World Bank (2011), women's skills in household affairs, which refer to their concern for their husbands, indicate women's attitudes and behavior outside the home, such as in sales and administration.

Promotion through the Website

In mid-2017, the village government and BUMDes administrators began to look at the potential to develop the concept of a tourist village. In achieving long-term goals, BUMDes Sumber Sejahtera utilizes the village website as the spearhead of tourism promotion. The study findings show that BUMDes have a separate budget for website development and maintenance. The center for tourism village branding through the website indicates that BUMDes promotion is well conceptualized and mature. This website is associated with social media such as Instagram and Facebook as support. It aims to attract investors and other parties to build cooperation in line with the study of Adhibah et al. (2022), who explained that BUMDes Sumber Sejahtera utilizes social media Instagram with the account name Pujon Kidul and a web portal with the address http://pujonkidul-malangkab.desa.id as a promotional tool.

Study Limitations

This study is limited to highlighting how women contribute to the management of BUMDes. Hence, it does not emphasize on the perspective of feminism or aspects of the women's movement. Then this study is limited to the scope of information technology that has been developed so far without connecting with the Smart Village concept. This concept is inseparable from the content of the Village Law, which gave birth to the Village Fund to encourage the development of significant innovations to solve village administrative management problems (Saputra & Isnain, 2021; Yana et al., 2020). The Smart Village concept aims to pursue new opportunities related to digital technology, networks, and new services that support knowledge and innovative solutions for community business development (Renukapp et al., 2022).

Conclusions

Based on the presentation in this study, BUMDes provides a broader space for women to develop their capacities. In this sense, BUMDes does not only help economically for Village Original Income (PADes) but also provides a platform for women to be actively involved in the social strata in the non-domestic realm. The success of BUMDes in this study shows that women's participation can accelerate development from downstream. It is in line with the national development goals, which place gender equality as part of human resource development. Contextual preferences in the tourism industry provide a compass for rural economic development through BUMDes. One of these contexts is geographical areas such as marine tourism in Binor village and agricultural tourism in Pujon Kidul village. The role of women in BUMDes management in the two cases in this study differs in two respects. First, women's empowerment in Binor Village was initiated by the village head, while BUMDes in Pujon Kidul Village, women are directly involved in BUMDes institutions. Second, the BUMDes manager appoints a special team to manage the marketing promotion of BUMDes products and village tourism branding in Binor village. At the same time, Pujon Kidul Village utilizes the village website and promotional support from the Ministry of Tourism. The two BUMDes show that marketing promotion techniques do not only rely on conventional methods but also use modern information technology tools.

Practical Implications

This study is an open door to see the success of gender-based BUMDes management in two villages in the East Java region. This study helps developing information technology-based management models in rural areas, especially the role of women in managing village-owned enterprises.

This study helpful for identifying the long-term role of practitioners in the development of information technology as a basis for marketing business unit products under BUMDes, including the framework for the intelligent village.

References

Adelman, I., & Morris, C. T. (1973). *Social Equity and Economic Growth in Developing Countries*. Stanford, CA: Stanford University Press.

Adhibah, A., Alam, U. M., & Munandar, M. A. (2022). The role of local institutions in community empowerment: A study on the management of village owned enterprises in Pujonkidul, Malang Regency [in Indonesian]. *Sospol: Jurnal Sosial Politik*, 8(1), 122–132. https://doi.org/10.22219/jurnalsospol.v8i1.18685

Bagus, N. (2020). Strategy for development of village-owned enterprises (BUMDES) for private-owned enterprise cooperation [in Indonesian]. *JISIP: Jurnal Ilmu Sosial Dan Ilmu Politik*, 9(2), 98–101. https://doi.org/10.33366/jisip.v9i2.2226

Falk, A., & Hermle, J. (2018). Relationship of gender differences in preferences to economic development and gender equality. *Science*, 362(6412), eaas9899.

Hamidullah, M. F., Riccucci, N. M., & Pandey, S. K. (2015). Women in city hall: Gender dimensions of managerial values. *The American Review of Public Administration*, 45(3), 247–262. https://doi.org/10.1177/0275074013498464

Haryati, E., Nasikun, J., & Tjokrowinoto, M. (2020). Political configuration, policy character and poverty alleviation. *Jurnal Wacana Kinerja: Kajian Praktis-Akademis Kinerja dan Administrasi Pelayanan Publik*, 6(4), 43–56.

Ilham, I., Muttaqin, U. I., & Idris, U. (2020). Development of Bumkam based on local potential in the border area of Indonesia-Papua New Guinea [in Indonesian]. *Community Development Journal: Jurnal Pengabdian Masyarakat*, 1(2), 104–109. https://doi.org/10.31004/cdj.v1i2.722

Ismail, A. (2020). Growth and inequality of inter-regional economic development in West Kalimantan Province. *Pertumbuhan Dan Ketimpangan Pembangunan Ekonomi Anatar Daerah Fi Provinsi Kalimantan Barat*, 11, 143–159.

Kafabih, A. (2018). Analysis of the role of village-owned enterprises (Bum Desa) social capital on poverty alleviation [in Indonesian]. *OECONOMICUS Journal of Economics*, 3(1), 51–70. https://doi.org/10.15642/oje.2018.3.1.51-70

Lloyd, M. (2007). *Judith Butler: From norms to politics* (Vol. 20). Cambridge: Polity Press.

Ministry of Village. (2022). Building Village Index. Retrieved August 19, 2022, from https://idm.kemendesa.go.id/

Moleong, L. J. (2016). *Qualitative Research Methodology*. Bandung: PT. Teen Rosdakarya Offset.

Maulana, Y. S., Maulina, E., Kostini, N., & Herawati, T. (2022). Integration of electronic business on tourism: A bibliometric network analysis. *Journal of Environmental Management & Tourism*, 13(6), 1779–1797.

Mustangin, D. K., Islami, N. P., Setyaningrum, B., & Prasetyawati, E. (2017). Community empowerment based on local potential through the tourism village program in Bumiaji village [in Indonesian]. *Sosioglobal: Jurnal Pemikiran Dan Penelitian Sosiologi*, *2*(1), 59–72. https://doi.org/10.24198/jsg. v2i1.15282

Nasrulhaq, A. (2019, April 26). Until 2018, 61 percent of villages in Indonesia already have BUMDes [In Indonesian]. DetikNews. Retrieved August 19, 2022, from https://news.detik.com/berita/d-4526846/ hingga-2018-61-persen-desa-di-indonesia-sudah-punya-bumdes

Nurpuspita, R., Sarfiah, S. N., & Ratnasari, E. D. (2019). Analysis of village fund management as the realization of one of the goals of the Nawacita program "Building Indonesia from the periphery" in Bener District, Purworejo Regency in 2016 [in Indonesian]. *DINAMIC: Directory Journal of Economic*, *1*(2), 136–150. https://doi.org/10.31002/dinamic.v1i2.511

Nursan, M., & Utama-FR, A. F. (2019). Strategy for development of agriculture-based village owned enterprises (Bumdes) in West Sumbawa Regency [in Indonesian]. *Jurnal Social Economic of Agriculture*, *8*(2). https://doi.org/ 10.26418/j.sea.v8i2.37726

Nursetiawan, I. (2018). Independent village development strategy through BUMDES innovation [in Indonesian]. *MODERAT: Jurnal Ilmiah Ilmu Pemerintahan*, *4*(2), 72–81. https://doi.org/10.25147/moderat.v4i2.1488

Olsson, O., & Hibbs Jr, D. A. (2005). Biogeography and long-run economic development. *European Economic Review*, *49*(4), 909–938.

Probolinggo Regency Government. (2020, August 25). BUMDes Binor Energi is Nominated for the Top 6 East Java [In Indonesian]. Retrieved August 19, 2022, from https://probolinggokab.go.id/bumdes-binor-energi-masuk-nominasi-6-besar-jawa-timur/

Puspitawati, H. (2013). *Gender Concept, Theory and Analysis*. Bogor: Departe-men Ilmu Keluarga dan Kon-sumen Fakultas Ekologi Manusia Institut Pertanian.

Renukappa, S., Suresh, S., Abdalla, W., Shetty, N., Yabbati, N., & Hiremath, R. (2022). Evaluation of smart village strategies and challenges. *Smart and Sustainable Built Environment*, (ahead-of-print). https://doi.org/10.1108/ SASBE-03-2022-0060

Rohim, Asmuni, A., & Muttaqin, M. Z. (2021). Multi-sector collaboration: Success stories of tourism village development. *Jurnal Ilmiah Ilmu Administrasi Publik*, *11*(2), 395–410. https://doi.org/10.26858/jiap.v11i2.26293

Saputra, M. A., & Isnain, A. R. (2021). Application of smart village in improving community services using web engineering method (case study: Desa Sukanegri Jaya) [in Indonesian]. *Jurnal Teknologi Dan Sistem Informasi (JTSI)*, *2*(3), 49–55. Retrieved August 21, 2022, from http://jim.teknokrat.ac.id/index. php/JTSI

Siagan, A. O. (2021). Analysis of development of village owned enterprises (BUMDes) Harapan Oesena in Oesena village, Amarasi District, Kupang Regency [in Indonesian]. *JRE: Jurnal Riset Entrepreneurship*, *4*(1), 33–43. https://doi.org/10.30587/jre.v4i1.2221

Sonowal, M. K. (2013). Impact of education in women empowerment: A case study of SC and ST women of Sonitpur District, Assam. *International Journal of Computer Applications in Engineering Sciences, 3*, 27. Retrieved August 23, 2022, from https://citeseerx.ist.psu.edu/viewdoc/download?doi=10.1.1.303.2672 &rep=rep1&type=pdf

Suci, Y. R. (2017). The development of MSMEs (micro, small and medium enterprises) in Indonesia [in Indonesian]. *Cano Economos, 6*(1), 51–58. Retrieved August 23, 2022, from https://journal.upp.ac.id/index.php/cano/article/view/627

Sulaksana, J., & Nuryanti, I. (2019). Strategy for development of village owned enterprises (BUMDes) case in Bumdes Mitra Sejahtera, Cibunut village, Argapura District, Majalengka Regency [in Indonesian]. *Jurnal Ekonomi Pertanian Dan Agribisnis (JEPA), 3*(2), 348–359. https://doi.org/10.21776/ub.jepa.2019.003.02.11

Sulistyastuti, D. R. (2004). Dinamika Usaha Kecil dan Menengah (UKM) Analisis Konsentrasi Regional UKM di Indonesia 1999–2001. *Economic Journal of Emerging Markets, 9*(2), 143–164. https://doi.org/10.20885/ejem.v9i2.617

Termine, P., & Percic, M. (2015). Rural women's empowerment through employment from the Beijing platform for action onwards. *IDS Bulletin, 46*(4), 33–40. https://doi.org/10.1111/1759-5436.12154

Utami, N. V., Rofieq, A., & Rahayu, S. D. (2022). The role of village-owned enterprises (Bumdes) Sumber Sejahtera Pujon Kidul Malang Regency in improving community welfare. *KYBERNAN: Jurnal Ilmiah Ilmu Pemerintahan, 13*(1), 1–6. https://doi.org/10.33558/kybernan.v13i1.4525

Wahab, D. A., Puspitawati, L., Supriyati, S., Purfini, A. P., & Yulianto, H. D. (2022). Improved governance and competence of Bumdes and IRT in Pagerwangi village Lembang through the smart asset application [in Indonesian]. *E-Dimas: Jurnal Pengabdian kepada Masyarakat, 13*(2), 249–253. https://doi.org/10.26877/e-dimas.v13i2.4928

World Bank, World Development Report. (2012). Gender Equality and Development, The International Bank for Reconstruction and Development/World Bank, Washington D.C. 2011. https://doi.org/10.1596/978-0-8213-8810-5

Yana, S., Gunawan, R. D., & Budiman, A. (2020). Information system for village financial distribution services for development (case study: Dusun Srikaya) [in Indonesian]. *Jurnal Informatika Dan Rekayasa Perangkat Lunak, 1*(2), 254–263. https://doi.org/10.33365/jatika.v1i2.621

Chapter 5

Being a Female Gig Worker on a Food Delivery Service Platform

Obed Kwame Adzaku Penu
University of Ghana Business School, University of Ghana, P O Box LG 78, Legon, Ghana

Joseph Budu
School of Technology, Ghana Institute of Management and Public Administration, Ghana, P. O. Box AH50 Achimota, Ghana

Thomas Anning-Dorson
School of Business Sciences, University of the Witwatersrand, CLM Building, First Floor, Office P7, Braamfontein Campus West, Johannesburg, South Africa

Richard Boateng
University of Ghana Business School, University of Ghana, P O Box LG 78, Legon, Ghana

Contents

Introduction

The gig economy can be broadly defined as a labor market where online platforms connect service providers offering temporary and flexible labor services to consumers in need of those services for a fee determined by online platforms (Anwar & Graham, 2021; Biswas & Bathla, 2022). Having emerged as a new avenue for work and employment, the gig economy has experienced exponential growth in the last decades, thereby redefining the nature of work and contributing to a significant change in the organization of contemporary economies (Healy et al., 2017). Representative sectors in the gig economy include ride-sharing (e.g., via platforms such as Uber and Bolt), food delivery services (e.g., through platforms such as Glovo, Bolt Food, Jumia Food, and Deliveroo), as well as translation, transcription, video editing, or graphic design (via platforms such as 99 Designs, Fiverr, and Upwork).

Despite the growing popularity of gig work and the rapid growth of the gig economy worldwide, previous research seeking to understand women's participation in gig economy has been scarce (Barzilay, 2018; Churchill et al., 2019). To fill this gap in the literature, this chapter focuses on the physical gig economy – i.e., the sector where gig workers meet up with consumers to deliver tasks assigned to them through an online gig platform. Not aiming to provide a comprehensive account of the experiences of all women engaged in gig work in Ghana, we focus on providing an in-depth analysis of the experience of one of such woman who works in Ghana's gig economy. Accordingly, this chapter reports the results of a small-scale qualitative investigation of both positive and negative experiences of a female gig worker in Ghana. The results of our qualitative case study are intended to draw the attention of academics, policymakers, practitioners, and the general public to the gender aspects of gig work.

In the next section, we present a case study of Diana, a female Bolt Food Delivery Platform worker. This is followed by some reflections that can be derived from the results of our study. The chapter concludes with the formulation of several questions to be explored in further research.

Diana, the Female Bolt Food Delivery Platform Worker

Profile

Diana, 23 years old and a single mother of one, has been delivering food to customers through the Bolt Food platform in Ghana's capital Accra. She has been working on the platform since September 2021. On moving in 2018 from Paga in the Upper East Region of Ghana to Ghana's capital Accra to make a living, Diana currently stays in a rented single room at Madina Estate, a suburb of Accra, with her sister and daughter. Diana's dependents include her daughter and sister, as well as her mother and siblings who remained in Paga. All of them look up to her in times of need.

The support she provides to her dependents is financial (e.g., supporting her relatives with money to buy food, medicines, etc.). Diana has a Junior High School (JHS) certificate and has not continued her education since she finished JHS. On finishing high school, Diana first enrolled as an apprentice seamstress, but later dropped out because of the lack of financial support during the training process. Of the 3 years of apprentice training, she managed to finish only 1 year (Figure 5.1).

Prior Work

On moving to Accra in 2018 and before joining Bolt Food in 2021, Diana worked as a full-time waitress in a restaurant in Accra. However, work conditions there were not good: not only did she and her colleagues regularly experience verbal abuse by the restaurant owner, but her earnings as a waitress were not enough to cover her basic needs. She shared the following description of her experience:

> The woman I worked for at the restaurant was not treating us the workers well – almost every day she would find a reason to insult us, so I decided to quit the job. She was paying us GHc 400.00 a month. Imagine this country and living on GHc 400.00 a month.

Figure 5.1 Diana on her motorbike riding to work. (Source: Fieldwork Data.)

Diana's first attempt at finding a job after she left her previous job was joining the popular male-dominated Okada business. Okada is a motorcycle serving as a taxi, with passengers sitting behind the driver. However, in this work environment, Diana faced a lot of resistance from the men who were frequently hostile toward her and did not want her to join them. Dian provided the following account of her experiences at the Okada waiting points (Figure 5.2):

> When I started, I wanted to do Okada. But when I went close to the men at the place where we waited for passengers, they didn't want me near them. Some of them told me the work was not for women, so I should stop. So, I had no option but to stop because, already, I left the restaurant because I was not happy, so there was no point in being in another place where I would not be happy because the people there didn't want me in their midst.

Why Join Bolt Food?

On facing a hostile reception in the Okada work environment, Diana was introduced to Bolt Food by her sister who was also doing deliveries via the

Figure 5.2 Okada riders waiting for passengers. (Source: Graphic Online (2018).)

Bolt Food platform. Being a woman, and knowing that the food delivery space could be ventured into by women like herself or her sister motivated Diana. With her experience in motorbike riding – which is the main means of commuting for many residents of the northern part of Ghana – Diana had no difficulties in starting to work in an industry that required one to have motorbike riding skills. As she described it:

> I didn't have to learn to ride a bike because in the north one of the main means of transportation (even for women) was motorbikes, so I already knew how to ride one.

Sign-Up Process

Diana's sister was not only a source of encouragement and motivation for Diana but also helped her to get a motorbike from a friend to start working. The platform requirement for her to join the platform was to show evidence of having a motorbike. As a biker, Diana also needed to provide a license registration for the motorbike, as well as a registered telephone contact. Together with other volunteers undergoing the sign-up process, Diana took a day's orientation at Bolt Food to familiarize herself with the delivery process. Interestingly, however, the platform did not require any school certificate from workers to enroll them – accordingly, Diana's inability to acquire a Senior high school certificate, which is usually the minimum educational certificate needed to get a job in Ghana, did not affect her sign-up to the platform.

As Diana said:

> As for Bolt Food, they take people every day. Each day we see new people joining. You don't need any certificate, you just need to know how to express yourself in English, even if it's broken English, they will take you, and that's why you see many of the young guys joining.

Typical Day

Diana's day as a Bolt Food delivery worker starts at 9 a.m. and ends at about 7 p.m. However, due to her responsibilities as a single mother, she sometimes starts working at 11 a.m. She usually wakes up at dawn (at about 5 a.m.) to make sure her daughter has everything ready for the day ahead and then leaves home for work. Unlike her male colleagues who mostly start working at about 7 a.m., Diana's responsibilities as a mother influence how much she can make for the day: namely, starting work later than her male colleagues negatively affects her earnings. Along with having to start later, Diana is also compelled to close earlier than her male co-workers, as she has to look after her child.

> I wake up at about 5 a.m. but I start work at 9 a.m. because of my daughter, if she has to go to school, I prepare her for school. Sometimes I can even delay in starting work because of my daughter, so I sometimes start at 11 a.m., prepare food for her and do some washing before I prepare to work for the day. And the work that we do, you have to be online to deliver before you can get paid, so if you don't start work early, it means you lose money. The closing time too, because of my daughter I can't work late – I need to go back home to take care of her – as for the men, some can even work late till 11 p.m.

Along with child-rearing duties, other Diana's responsibilities include cleaning her bike. Her usual pickup and delivery location are in the East Legon enclave where there are many university campuses and restaurants. On a typical day, she does between 8 and 10 deliveries. Some days can be bad and, as a woman, Diana sometimes feels this is not the right job, because she fails to make enough earnings on the platform. In order to make up for the shortfall in her earnings via the platform, Diana has resorted to doing personal deliveries for people off the platform. As she described this:

> Sometimes, I do personal deliveries outside the app – so, for example, if someone I know wants me to deliver something for them, they just call me and, if I'm available, I deliver for them, because now there are so many riders on Bolt, and it has reduced the [number of] orders that we get.

In order to get orders, Diana strategically positions herself at locations in the enclave where she works. These locations are usually at the entrance of restaurants.

> Two weeks ago, I was at KFC East Legon, and last week I moved to Opkonglo [adjacent to the University of Ghana Campus], there is a restaurant there known as FT. Now I'm at A&C Mall, there is a popular restaurant there known as Nima Chow.

How Breaks Are Spent

Diana takes no deliberate breaks whiles working. She carries food in her backpack and eats when restaurants are not ready with a pickup. Sometimes when she is close to home in the afternoons, she goes home to eat, as buying food outside is more expensive. She also uses this opportunity to see her daughter if she is back from school. As Diana said:

> I don't go on breaks, because with this job, you have to work all the time before you can earn enough for the day. But sometimes when I'm close to the house, I just pass by and eat something, but most of the time I have food in my bag so when I'm at the restaurant and they are delaying, I just eat.

High and Low Moments

In Diana's work routine, there are both high and low moments. The high moment for Diana is her ability to earn enough through the platform to take care of her needs and those of her daughter. She is happy when she gets tips from customers, many of whom get surprised to see a female delivery worker. She is also happy to engage in social interactions with colleague male drivers: "as riders, we are able to meet to chit-chat." She is also happy that, unlike in the Okada space where she suffered from gender stereotyping, working in the platform-mediated space has removed those barriers and now she can interact with other (predominantly male) workers in this new working environment.

Comparing her previous work as a waitress in a restaurant where she suffered from verbal abuse from the business owner, Diana finds the situation to be different – although, at times, customers can be difficult, she is definitely better off now. Yet the days when she gets worried are when her bike gives her problems, which entails that she is unable to work.

She also dislikes the days when customers are rude, which gets her down:

> Some customers can talk to you anyhow and then report you on top – and then the Bolt blocks you without even listening to your side of the issue.

Outcome and Impact

Earnings

Although Diana manages to put food on the table, she has not been able to consistently save from her earnings, as most of her earnings go into taking care of herself, her daughter, and her sister who lives with them and helps Diana to take care of her daughter. As mentioned previously, Diana manages to do between 8 and 10 deliveries in a day. She complained that, two weeks after she joined Bolt, the company reduced the rate per delivery from GHc 10.00 to GHc 9.00, which negatively affected her earnings:

> The initial agreement that short distances within 3 km was GHc 10.00 was then reduced to GHc9.00. The situation is even worse

now, as a rider can travel as far as 8 km or even sometimes 9 km and be given GHc 9.00. Meanwhile, the initial rate was within the range of 3 km for GHc 10.0. All of a sudden, they changed everything – and now we riders are worse off. Earlier on, with long distances (such as 4 km and above), we could earn between GHc18.00 and GHc25.00. But now we get just GHc9.00 and sometimes from GHc11.00 to GHc 18.00 for that. So, you end up spending more fuel for the same price.

Financial Infrastructure

While Diana is able to provide for herself and her dependents through her earnings, she has been unable to secure any loans with her earnings as collateral for the loan. However, she has opened a savings account where she deposits some of her earnings:

> There is not much to save to do anything – recently I opened a savings account with Fidelity bank, but I'm not able to put much in there – I have also opened another Susu account with Best Point, but there is no money there. Sometimes for a whole month, I haven't saved anything – the last time I did a deposit was three weeks ago. Specifically, I decided to open a saving account with Best Point to be able to get loans – but I haven't been able to engage them on that yet.

Empowerment

Diana feels empowered because she works when she wants. Also, having almost completed the re-payment for her "work and pay" motorbike, she is currently on her way to owning the bike. As a single mother, she manages to pay her rent and cater for her basic needs, as well as those of her daughter and sister. Therefore, she does not have to depend on a man for her living. As Diana described her situation,

> My daughter's father does not even take care of us, so it's the money I earn that takes care of us. Imagine me as a woman who has just a JHS certificate – what sort of work can I get in the formal sector? These days even graduates don't earn much, not to talk of me who is a JHS graduate. Some women earn a maximum of GHc

600.00 in a month, some GHc 500.00 or even GHc 350.00 – but here I am, a JHS leaver can even earn more than that in a month. Not forgetting that some of these women are required to work in eight-to-five jobs – and they are not independent in their job times like I am, [which is important], especially for mothers.

Diana also compares her situation as a delivery worker to those of women working in the formal sector and feels empowered by having the time on her hands to take care of her daughter. As she phrased it:

As a single mother, imagine working in a bank or an office. I may only be given 3 months of maternity leave – after that, I need to find someone to take care of my child – but working on Bolt, I have all the time to take care of the daughter and still be able to go to work when I want but still put food on the table and get money for my upkeep.

Furthermore, although the platform has no formally recognized policies for women, Diana recounts situations where dispatchers have been considerate in reassigning her late-hour deliveries to men because the locations were no-go areas even for men. She said:

I remember another instance where I pleaded with a dispatcher to re-assign a delivery I was supposed to do to another rider because it was late and the location was not all that safe and he did – though, ideally, riders are not supposed to reject any delivery location that they are given, but I believe he did that because I was a woman and needed to be safe – so he re-assigned it to a man.

Diana also feels empowered because of being able to develop her own delivery business. This was something she was able to slowly start through the networks she had established while doing deliveries and using her savings from working on the Bolt Food platform. Diana provided the following description of her nascent business (Figure 5.3):

Through the Bolt Food work, I'm putting plans in place to start my own delivery business – it is called 'Diana's Delivery Service'.

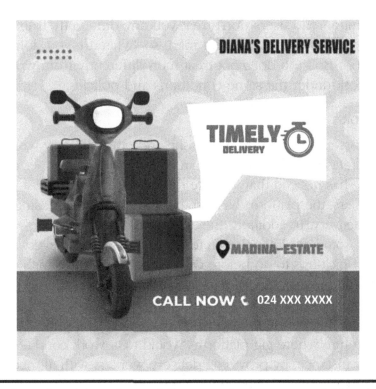

Figure 5.3 Flyer advertising Diana's delivery services. (Source: Fieldwork data.)

I used the money that I saved from the work and also when I'm delivering on Bolt, some people whom I meet take my number and when they have deliveries, they call me to do it for them.

Unintended Consequences

The continuous growth of fuel prices – which changes overnight at a high rate – is an important concern for Diana:

Just a couple of days ago, I bought a gallon of fuel for GHc 42.00; now it has gone to GHc 45.00

Another difficulty for Diana is that she did not expect work conditions for women to be the same as those of men. Gig platforms do not have any policies that give special consideration to women, so she has to work under the same conditions as her male peers. Based on this experience, Diana thinks that gig platforms are not paying enough attention to gender-related issues. As she said:

As a woman, road users don't treat you any differently from men, because to them the work is for men, so "what are you doing in a man's job?". Bolt too does not treat men differently from women; we all work under the same conditions and policies.

Future Outlook

Diana looks forward to a future where she and other delivery workers would receive increments per order, rather than have their earnings per delivery increased. She has noticed that, despite the increment in the cost per delivery for the customers, the platform has done nothing about increasing the amount they get per delivery. In addition, she anticipates a future where women would receive some consideration in terms of pick-up or delivery location and the number of pick-ups to do before earning bonuses. In Diana's opinion, platforms should provide special packages to women in order to motivate more women to join platform work. An example of a special dispensation could include selling motorbikes to women at subsidized prices. Diana also anticipates a future where gig platforms would treat work conditions more seriously – for instance, by providing delivery workers with all necessary safety gear and equipment needed for work.

As she said:

> We need raincoats, boots, and elbow and knee guards so that, if there are accidents, we can at least feel protected.

Reflections from the Study

The reflections outlined below provide guidelines for researchers studying women's participation in the gig economy.

- The gig economy has promoted women's participation in labor sectors that have previously been reserved for men.
- Women can earn relatively more from gig work as compared to their earnings from 'some' regular jobs.
- Women are frequently constrained by their family duties (i.e., taking care of their underage children), which adversely affects the number of hours they work and, as a result, their earnings as gig workers.
- Today's gig platforms do not offer special treatment to women; in instances where such consideration is given, the decision is left to the discretion of platform dispatchers.

■ As evidenced by Diana's ability to set up her own delivery business from her gig earnings and her ability to pay her rent and support herself and her daughter, women feel financially and economically empowered by the earnings they make as gig workers.

■ Female gig workers are not immune to vulnerabilities, as they are frequently lured into situations that make them vulnerable to attacks and harassment.

■ Urgent attention by government labor agencies is required to enforce decent working conditions and protection for gig workers, whiles maximizing opportunities being offered through these platforms.

Questions for Discussion

The following questions should be addressed in further research:

1. How do female gig workers overcome the challenges that they face in the gig economy?
2. How do female gig workers deal with the constraints imposed by their family responsibilities to ensure they fully participate in the gig economy? Actors use social media to mitigate vulnerability effects, enhance livelihood assets or diversify livelihood strategies?
3. How does the gig economy contribute to the inclusion and/or exclusion of female gig workers?
4. What is the role of gig platforms in ensuring the full participation of female workers in the gig economy?

Definitions of Terms

A&C Mall – a popular shopping mall located in East Legon.

East Legon – a popular suburb in Accra, Ghana's capital, known to be home to local elite. The suburb is also known to be home to many universities.

GHc – Ghana cedi, the currency used in Ghana.

The gig economy – a labor market where online platforms connect service providers offering temporary and flexible labor services to consumers in need of those services for a fee determined by online platforms.

Gig worker – a person who works in the gig economy. These persons subscribe to online gig platforms to offer services (popular among these services in Ghana are ride-hailing and food delivery).

JHS – Junior High School. The level of education between primary school and senior high school and attended by children aged 13–15 years old.

KFC – a popular fast-food restaurant in Ghana.

Nima Chow – a popular restaurant located in the enclave of Ghana's international airport, Kotoka International Airport.

Okada – a motorcycle serving as a taxi, with passengers sitting behind the driver.

Opkonglo – a suburb in Accra, Ghana's capital (adjacent to the University of Ghana Campus).

Paga – a popular town in the Upper East Region in the Northern part of Ghana.

The physical gig economy – a sector of the gig economy where gig workers meet up with consumers to deliver the tasks assigned to them via the online gig platform.

University of Ghana – The oldest and largest of 25 public universities in Ghana. It is located in East Legon.

References

Anwar, M. A., & Graham, M. (2021). Between a rock and a hard place: Freedom, flexibility, precarity and vulnerability in the gig economy in Africa. *Competition & Change, 25*(2), 237–258. https://doi.org/10.1177/1024529420914473

Barzilay, A. R. (2018). Discrimination without discriminating: Learned gender inequality in the labour market and gig economy. *Cornell Journal of Law and Public Policy, 28*, 545–567.

Biswas, D., & Bathla, P. (2022). A study on relationship between unemployment and rise of the Gig Economy. *Asian Journal of Management, 13*(1), 77–84. https://doi.org/10.52711/2321-5763.2022.00014

Churchill, B., Ravn, S., & Craig, L. (2019). Gendered and generational inequalities in the gig economy era. *Journal of Sociology, 55*(4), 627–636. https://doi.org/10.1177/1440783319893754

Healy, J., Nicholson, D., & Pekarek, A. (2017). Should we take the gig economy seriously? *Labour & Industry, 27*(3), 232–248. https://doi.org/10.1080/10301763.2017.1377048

Chapter 6

Gender Digital Divide in India: Examining the Reality and Bridging the Gap

Lalit Anjana

Faculty of Law, University of Delhi, 1656, Sector 10A, Gurugram, Haryana, India

Contents

Introduction

The pursuit of gender parity is about ensuring that women's rights are protected and building a sustainable, equitable economy that benefits everyone. Gender parity is crucial because it ensures that everyone, regardless of gender, has an equal opportunity to contribute to the advancement of our society and economy (Department for International Development, 2018). In the digital sphere, gender inequality is just as prevalent as it is in the actual world. The rate at which women use and get access to digital technology is much lower than men's (UNICEF, 2021). The majority of people throughout the globe (about 66%) now utilize the Internet to get information or use online services. An average of 62% of men, compared to 57% of women globally, use the Internet (Women in Digital Transformation LLC & DAKA advisory AB, 2022). Gender inequalities prevent us from attaining equality, and the gender digital divide is no exception (Chandra, 2022). The "digital divide" is the difference between those who have access, the necessary skills, and the aptitude to utilize information and communication technology and those who do not. Depending on variables such as gender, amount of education, employment position, and income, the digital divide may appear in various ways (Abu-Shanab & Al-Jamal, 2015). The term "Information and Communication Technology" (abbreviated as "ICT") refers to a wide range of technologies that enable the generation, management, and allow for exchange of information and communication. It also encompasses recent digital technologies like personal computers and the Internet (Purushothaman & Zhou, 2014). The gender digital gap is the chapter's primary focus, highlighting how women fall behind males in terms of accessing and using ICT (Rashid, 2016). In today's modern era, the gender gap in Internet access and other digital technologies impedes women's empowerment, and gender inequality has been a cause of worry for thousands of years (Rikowski, 2008). ICTs are undeniably effective and valuable for both men and women, and they are crucial for women's e-learning possibilities, gender parity, and women's empowerment. Women confront a number of societal and economic restrictions that make it difficult for them to use and access ICTs resources (Kwapong, 2009).

Gender norms in patriarchal nations like India and other developing nations hinder women's access to technology, particularly those from disadvantaged groups (Arun & Arun, 2021). Several factors contribute to the gender digital gap, such as inexperience with technology, poor rates of digital literacy, and unequal accessibility to computers and other electronic devices (Kwapong, 2009). Digital technologies directly connect individuals to the world (Davaki, 2018). Given the persisting gender disparities in the digital world and the rising recognition of digital technology as a tool for empowering women, many national and international organizations have supported efforts to promote gender parity in online participation and access (Kashyap et al., 2020).

Situation Faced

Gender norms firmly ingrained in patriarchal nations like India and other developing countries frequently hinder and impact fair access to the Internet and technology for women and girls, especially those from disadvantaged and resource-poor households. Various Reports show uneven access to the Internet and technological devices, lower digital literacy rates, and a lack of familiarity with digital technologies among females. Since India and other developing nations have been grappling with a growing digital divide for some time, it's no surprise that digital technology developments in developing countries are more sensitive to gender inequalities. The constraints of the offline world tend to spread into the online realm when it comes to females. Previous studies have shown that gender inequality causes and exacerbate the digital gap. This research stands out because it provides a detailed graphical representation of how economic, demographic, and other factors all play a role in perpetuating gender disparities in the digital world.

The purpose of this chapter is to examine the gender disparities in the area of ICT, as well as to determine the extent to which this problem exists and the reasons that contribute to it. In this study, a doctrinal research technique was applied. Data were acquired from several primary and secondary sources, including books, articles, journals, research papers, e-library resources, and national and international reports.

Operational Definitions

■ Gender digital divide: "Inequalities between men and women in the intensity of use of computer and internet connection as well as in the participation in the basic uses of internet and indicates that this kind of segregation could be measured through equality and ICT indicators" (Kerras et al., 2020, p. 2).

■ Gender Equality: "Gender equality is not a women's issue but should concern and fully engage men as well as women. Equality between women and men is seen both as a human rights issue and as a precondition for, and indicator of, sustainable people-centered development" (U.N. Women, 2021).

■ Gender Digital Divide Index: "It is a framework that provides a snapshot in time of the current state of gender digital gaps in countries to help decision-makers in government, business, civil society, and donor organizations gain a clearer understanding of the strengths, weaknesses and opportunities for action" (Women in Digital Transformation LLC & DAKA advisory AB, 2022, p. 3).

Right to Gender Neutrality in Internet Access

Human rights should be both a core assumption and a fundamental goal of Internet regulation, including steps to bridge the gender digital divide (United Nations High Commissioner for Human Rights, 2017). Constitutional obligations, rights, and guiding principles could be utilized to implement favorable policies that benefit women and bridge the gender gap in the digital space. Furthermore, the Internet aids citizens in voicing their thoughts worldwide; the constitutional provision that governs free speech in the area of the Internet is the fundamental right to speech and expression (Laxmikanth, 2022). Consequently, in the modern day, having easy access to the Internet is crucial for protecting one's rights.

> The fundamental role that freedom of opinion and expression plays in the ability of human to interact with society at large, in particular in the realms of economic and political participation and reaffirms that Active participation of women on equal terms with men at all levels of decision-making is essential to the achievement of equality, sustainable development, peace and democracy.
>
> **Faheema Shirin**
> *R.K v. State of Kerala (2019, Para 13)*

The Kerala High Court further ruled that there must be a mechanism to encourage and guarantee that all people have equal opportunity to utilize and benefit from ICTs. Furthermore, it was determined that women's constitutionally guaranteed rights, both offline and online, be safeguarded since women's involvement in all aspects of the country is critical for women's empowerment (Faheema Shirin. R.K v. State of Kerala, 2019). If women are restricted from accessing and using digital technologies and the Internet, this violates their right to equality. The CEDAW committee has emphasized the linkages between ICTs and gender bias, considering both women's uneven access to ICTs and the potential for ICTs to empower women.

> States Parties shall take all appropriate measures to eliminate discrimination against women in rural areas in order to ensure, on

a basis of equality of men and women, that they participate in and benefit from rural development and, in particular, shall ensure to such women the right: To obtain all types of training and education, formal and non-formal, including that relating to functional literacy, as well as, inter alia, the benefit of all community and extension services, in order to increase their technical proficiency.

Milani et al.
(2004, pp. 83, 84)

Sustainable Development Goal (SDG)

All women globally must be granted equal rights, opportunity, and freedom from prejudice. Goals for advancing women's empowerment via ICTs are included in the United Nations' Sustainable Development Goals (David & Phillips, 2022). Goal 5 of sustainable development goals (SDGs) recognizes that empowering women and achieving parity between the sexes is crucial to a nation's development and prosperity (United Nations, 2022). Discrimination against women has many underlying causes, both online and offline, and steps must be taken immediately to remedy them if we are to achieve gender equality in all spheres by the year 2030. Only then will all nations be able to realize the goal of achieving gender parity in all areas (United Nations, 2015). SDGs provide nations an opportunity to reduce the gender digital gap. India, as well as other developing nations that are members of the United Nations (U.N.), has also pledged to:

■ Target 1.4: "By 2030, ensure that all men and women, in particular the poor and the vulnerable, have equal rights to economic resources, as well as access to basic services, ownership and control over land and other forms of property, inheritance, natural resources, appropriate new technology, and financial services, including microfinance" (NITI Aayog, 2021, p. 74).
■ Target 5. b: "Enhance the use of enabling technology, in particular information and communications technology, to promote the empowerment of women" (NITI Aayog, 2021, p. 101).

According to reports published by NITI AYOG, India's progress toward attaining the gender parity outlined in Goal 5 of SDGs remains below

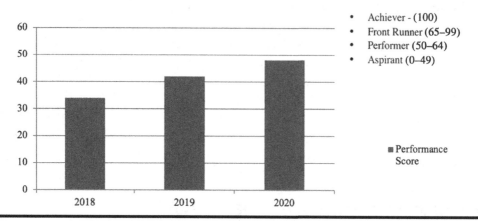

Figure 6.1   Sustainable Development Goal-5, goal-wise performance (NITI Aayog, 2018, 2019, 2021). (Source: NITI Aayog SDG India index reports.)

average (Figure 6.1). On the other hand, the performance index score in the area of gender equality is growing, but at a slow and steady rate, and the improvement is not significant. The relationship between technological advancement and women's rights is evident in SDG 5, as it seeks to encourage women's empowerment and equal rights. This goal includes the use of ICTs and other forms of technological advancement with the express purpose of empowering women (Mlambo-Ngcuka, 2017).

The struggle against gender inequality in the digital realm is greatly aided by using and accessing ICTs. It is on account of the fact that it provides "its users" with a means of achieving a better work-life balance by providing them with convenient access to resources and a variety of online educational, vocational, and career options. In addition, the advancement of technology presents women with a wide variety of chances for self-empowerment and other opportunities (Kerras et al., 2020). To realize the 2030 goal of SDG-Goal 5, it is also essential that the Internet is accessible to everyone globally.

Statistical Analysis

The facts and statistics for this part are obtained from the national family health survey-5 (NFHS-5) and GSMA, the mobile Gender Gap Report 2022, to quantitatively assess and illustrate the digital gender difference in India. NFHS-5 included, for the first time, information on male and female

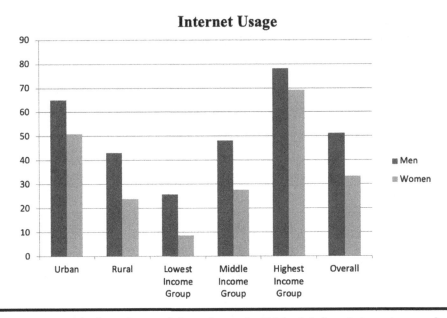

Figure 6.2   Graphical analyses of data shown in Table 6.1, i.e., Internet usage by men and women (age 15–49) based on selected background criteria. (Source: NFHS-5.)

Internet use throughout the nation. This research uses this secondary data to examine the gap between men and women regarding their use of and access to various forms of ICTs (Figure 6.2 and Table 6.1).

Data analysis: According to research, just 51% of women, in comparison to 65% of males in metropolitan areas of India, have ever accessed the Internet. On the other hand, Internet usage is far lower in rural parts of India, where only 24% of women and 43% of males have used the Internet. The gender disparity in Internet use is substantially more severe among those in the quintile with the lower average income than those in the quintile with the average income who have ever used the Internet. When we look at the overall general trend, we find that just 33 percent of women, compared to 51 percent of males, have used the Internet at some time in their life. Based on these findings, it is clear that there is a significant digital gender disparity; hence, immediate action must be taken to narrow this gap (Figure 6.3 and Table 6.2).

Data Analysis: According to the statistics, progress toward eliminating the gender divide in mobile Internet use has stalled. In contrast to women, whose percentage of mobile Internet usage remained stalled from 2020 to 2021, the percentage of Indian males who use the Internet on their mobile devices increased from 45% to 51% over this same period.

Table 6.1   In India, the Percentage of Women and Men between the Ages of 15 and 49 Who Have Ever Used the Internet, Depending on Their Demographic Background (2019–2021)

Background characteristic	Women (%)	Men (%)
Residence		
• Urban	51 (n = 34,839)	65 (n = 32,852)
• Rural	24 (n = 73,175)	43 (n = 60,291)
Wealth quintile		
• Lowest	8.6 (n = 19,904)	25.7 (n = 15,606)
• Middle	27.6 (n = 22,525)	48 (n = 19,829)
• Highest	69.2 (n = 21,432)	78.2 (n = 18,553)
Overall	33.3 (n = 108,014)	51.2 (n = 93,144)

Source: NFHS-5; International Institute for Population Sciences (IIPS) & ICF (2021, pp. 100–101).

Note: In the above table, the number of observations as per the category of men and women is depicted after percentage, and the number of observations per gender and category is denoted by "n".

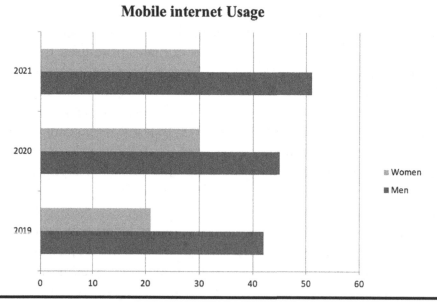

Figure 6.3   Graphical analysis of data as shown in Table 6.2. (Source: GSMA Consumer Surveys 2019, 2020, 2021.)

Table 6.2   Percentage of the Adult Population Using Mobile Internet in India Based on Gender, as Per GSMA Consumer Surveys

Year	Men (%)	Women (%)
2019	42	21
2020	45	30
2021	51	30

Source: GSMA Consumer Surveys 2019, 2020, and 2021; Shanahan (2022).

Practical Implications

The findings demonstrate that significant barriers to the gender digital divide in India and other developing countries, affecting women disproportionately, are location, education, and wealth. These variables have a more substantial impact on women than men. Findings further reveal that women's access to and usage of digital technology and the Internet remains lower than men's, even when women are educated, have sufficient income, and reside in urban areas. However, this disparity becomes much more prominent, and the gap increases when women have lower levels of education, lower incomes, and reside in rural regions. Complex socioeconomic factors negatively impact women's participation in the digital realm in India and other developing countries. As per findings, it can be concluded that the gender digital divide is greatly affected by proximate factors such as education, wealth, and locality, but these factors are insufficient to completely explain the obstacles that prevent India and other developing countries from achieving complete gender parity in the usage of digital technologies.

According to the findings of several different research organizations, it is abundantly apparent that gender disparities exist in digital arenas in India and other developing countries (Organisation for Economic Co-operation and Development, 2018). The gendered digital gap prevents women from receiving government social security benefits and accessing services such as reserving COVID-19 immunization appointments (Nikore & Uppadhayay, 2021). Access to and use of modern ICTs is like a double-edged sword. On the one hand, it helps to move society forward, but on the other, it makes the gender and social divides that already exist even bigger. Because of this, ICTs have the potential to both make gender inequality worse and fix it. Unfortunately, many women still can't use ICTs because they can't afford them, don't know how to use them, live in rural areas, or don't have the appropriate technical infrastructure (Brimacombe & Skuse, 2013). In India and other developing nations, the gender gap in access to digital technology is expected to endure *indefinitely* until it is adequately addressed. Besides economic considerations, societal and cultural factors also contribute to the gender digital gap (Potnis, 2016). Therefore, in India and other developing nations, there is an immediate need for policy formulations and frameworks prioritizing women's digital empowerment. The gender digital barrier must be bridged, and we all have an active role in that process.

Recommendations

The gender gap in the digital realm is undeniably a complicated and multifaceted issue. Consequently, no single solution or policy can address all the issues (David & Phillips, 2022; Larsson et al., 2019). Therefore, in addition to policy reforms, cooperation is needed across various initiatives aimed at bridging the digital gender divide. That is, gender equality in the digital sphere is a global problem that must be addressed not just through legislation but also by altering social and cultural attitudes and raising awareness.

- Passing digital regulations that enable public-private collaborations may help make the Internet more accessible and affordable for the public. In addition, to promote gender equality in Internet usage, the government should invest in Internet service providers rather than relying exclusively on private businesses to provide access (Sanders & Scanlon, 2021).
- Providing women with the knowledge, education, support, and financial resources they need in order to take advantage of the possibilities given by today's contemporary digital technologies (Perifanou & Economides, 2020).
- Regulations and policies governing net neutrality and Internet infrastructure must be framed in such a manner that they prioritize closing the gender digital gap (Sanders & Scanlon, 2021).
- Facilitating women's access to mobile technology and the Internet by offering free or discounted smart devices to women primarily from rural regions who have poor income levels and lack access to higher education through government grants.

- The government should make efforts to educate and train women using digital technology by developing specialized educational programs and training courses, especially those relevant to their economic activities.
- Governments must invest in developing villages with high-speed network connectivity that is both cheap and accessible.

Conclusion

This study demonstrates a gender digital gap, which must be addressed immediately. Women must have safe and equitable online spaces to express themselves and gain access to new opportunities and resources available in the digital realm. The chapter examines the existing gender digital divide and strategies for closing it in India and other developing countries. The findings show that the gender digital divide is a complex issue influenced by various socioeconomic factors. The most prudent course of action now is implementing policies, changing cultural attitudes, and raising awareness to help women become more tech-savvy and gain equal access to essential digital technologies.

References

Abu-Shanab, E., & Al-Jamal, N. (2015). Exploring the gender digital divide in Jordan. *Gender, Technology and Development, 19*(1), 91–113. https://doi.org/10.1177/0971852414563201

Arun, S., & Arun, T. (2021). Cracking it: Negotiating working-class gender capital through group enterprises in India. *Work, Employment and Society.* https://doi.org/10.1177/09500170211054951

Brimacombe, T., & Skuse, A. (2013). Gender, ICTs, and indicators: Measuring inequality and change. *Gender, Technology and Development, 17*(2), 131–157. https://doi.org/10.1177/0971852413488713

Chandra, A. (2022). Bridging the digital gender divide: Prerequisite for women empowerment. In S. Bala & P. Singhal (Eds.), *Gender Perspectives on Industry 4.0 and the Impact of Technology on Mainstreaming Female Employment* (pp. 31–32), essay. IGI Global Publisher of Timely Knowledge.

Davaki, K. (2018). (rep.). *The underlying causes of the digital gender gap and possible solutions for enhanced digital inclusion of women and girls.* Retrieved May 12, 2022, from https://www.europarl.europa.eu/RegData/etudes/STUD/2018/604940/IPOL_STU(2018)604940_EN.pdf

David, R., & Phillips, T. (2022). The gender digital gap: Shifting the theoretical focus to systems analysis and feedback loops. *Information, Communication & Society*, 1–17. https://doi.org/10.1080/1369118x.2022.2069507

Department for International Development. (2018). (rep.). *DFID Strategic Vision for Gender Equality A Call to Action for Her Potential, Our Future.* Retrieved April 27, 2022, from https://assets.publishing.service.gov.uk/government/uploads/system/uploads/attachment_data/file/708116/Strategic-vision-gender-equality1.pdf

Faheema Shirin. R.K v. State of Kerala, W.P (C). No. 19716/2019 L. (2019). Retrieved June 22, 2022, from https://www.livelaw.in/pdf_upload/pdf_upload-364655.pdf

International Institute for Population Sciences (IIPS) & ICF. (2022). (rep.). *National family health survey (NFHS-5), 2019–21: INDIA: volume I.* Retrieved May 19, 2022, from https://dhsprogram.com/pubs/pdf/FR375/FR375.pdf

Kashyap, R., Fatehkia, M., al Tamime, R., & Weber, I. (2020). Monitoring global digital gender inequality using the online populations of Facebook and Google. *Demographic Research*, *43*, 779–816. https://doi.org/10.4054/demres.2020.43.27

Kerras, H., Sánchez-Navarro, J. L., López-Becerra, E. I., & de-Miguel Gómez, M. D. (2020). The impact of the gender digital divide on sustainable development: Comparative analysis between the European Union and the Maghreb. *Sustainability*, *12*(8), 3347. https://doi.org/10.3390/su12083347

Kwapong, O. A. (2009). A comparison of ICT knowledge and usage among female distance learners in endowed and deprived communities of a developing country. *E-Learning and Digital Media*, *6*(2), 164–174. https://doi.org/10.2304/elea.2009.6.2.164

Larsson, A., Teigland, R., & Viitaoja, Y. (2019). Identifying the digital gender divide. In *The Digital Transformation of Labor (Open Access): Automation, the Gig Economy and Welfare* (pp. 235–253). Routledge.

Laxmikanth, M. (2022). *Indian Polity, 6th Edition [Paperback].* McGraw Hill India.

Milani, L. R., Albert, S. C., & Purushotma, K. (2004). *CEDAW: The treaty for the rights of women: Rights that benefit the entire community.* Working Group on Ratification of the U.N. Convention on the Elimination of All Forms of Discrimination Against Women.

Mlambo-Ngcuka, P. (2017, July 14). *Reshaping the Future: Women, Girls, ICTs and the SDGs.* United Nations. Retrieved July 22, 2022, from https://www.unwomen.org/en/news/stories/2017/7/reshaping-the-future-icts-and-the-sdgs

Nikore, M., & Uppadhayay, I. (2021, September 9). *India's Gendered Digital Divide: How the Absence of Digital Access Is Leaving Women Behind.* ORF. Retrieved May 22, 2022, from https://www.orfonline.org/expert-speak/indias-gendered-digital-divide/

NITI Aayog. (2018). (rep.). *SDG India Index, Baseline Report* (pp. 63–72). New Delhi, Delhi: Government of India. Retrieved from https://www.niti.gov.in/sites/default/files/2020-07/SDX_Index_India_Baseline_Report_21-12-2018.pdf

NITI Aayog. (2019). (rep.). *SDG India Index & Dashboard 2019–20* (pp. 69–79). New Delhi, Delhi: Government of India. Retrieved from https://www.niti.gov. in/sites/default/files/SDG-India-Index-2.0_27-Dec.pdf

NITI Aayog. (2021). (rep.). *SDG INDIA Index & Dashboard 2020–21 Partnerships in the Decade of Action* (pp. 101–107). New Delhi, Delhi: Government of India. Retrieved from https://sdgindiaindex.niti.gov.in/assets/Files/SDG3.0_ Final_04.03.2021_Web_Spreads.pdf

Organisation for Economic Co-operation and Development. (2018). (rep.). *Bridging the digital gender divide include, upskill, innovate.* Retrieved July 12, 2022, from https://www.oecd.org/digital/bridging-the-digital-gender-divide.pdf

Perifanou, M. A., & Economides, A. A. (2020). Gender digital divide in Europe. *International Journal of Business, Humanities and Technology, 10*(4). https:// doi.org/10.30845/ijbht.v10n4p2

Potnis, D. (2016). Inequalities creating economic barriers to owning mobile phones in India. *Information Development, 32*(5), 1332–1342. https://doi. org/10.1177/0266666915605163

Purushothaman, A., & Zhou, C. (2014). Change toward a creative society in developing contexts—Women's barriers to learning by information and communication technology. *Gender, Technology and Development, 18*(3), 363–386. https://doi.org/10.1177/0971852414544008

Rashid, A. T. (2016). Digital inclusion and social inequality: Gender differences in ICT access and use in five developing countries. *Gender, Technology and Development, 20*(3), 306–332. https://doi.org/10.1177/0971852416660651

Rikowski, R. (2008). Computers/information and communications technology, the information profession and the gender divide: Where are we going? *Policy Futures in Education, 6*(4), 482–506. https://doi.org/10.2304/ pfie.2008.6.4.482

Sanders, C. K., & Scanlon, E. (2021). The digital divide is a human rights issue: Advancing social inclusion through social work advocacy. *Journal of Human Rights and Social Work, 6*(2), 130–143. https://doi.org/10.1007/ s41134-020-00147-9

Shanahan, M. (2022). (rep.). *The Mobile Gender Gap Report 2022* (pp. 45–46). LondonUK: GSM Association. Retrieved July 12, 2022, from https://www. gsma.com/r/wp-content/uploads/2022/06/The-Mobile-Gender-Gap-Report-2022.pdf

UNICEF. (2021). (rep.). *Using big data for insights into the gender digital divide for girls: A discussion paper.* Retrieved June 17, 2022, from https://www.unicef.org/ eap/media/8326/file/%20Using%20big%20data%20for%20insights%20into%20 the%20gender%20digital%20divide%20for%20girls:%20A%20discussion%20 paper%20%20%20.pdf

United Nations. (2015). (rep.). *Transforming our world: the 2030 Agenda for Sustainable Development (A/RES/70/1).* Retrieved May 16, 2022, from https:// www.un.org/en/development/desa/population/migration/generalassembly/ docs/globalcompact/A_RES_70_1_E.pdf

United Nations. (2022). *Gender Equality and women's Empowerment.* United Nations Sustainable Development Goals. Retrieved July 25, 2022, from https://www.un.org/sustainabledevelopment/gender-equality/

United Nations High Commissioner for Human Rights. (2017). (rep.). *Promotion, protection and enjoyment of human rights on the Internet: ways to bridge the gender digital divide from a human rights perspective.* Retrieved June 12, 2022, from https://documents-dds-ny.un.org/doc/UNDOC/GEN/G17/111/81/PDF/G1711181.pdf?OpenElement

U.N. Women. (2021, August). *Gender Mainstreaming – A Strategy for Promoting Gender Equality.* United Nations. Retrieved July 12, 2022, from https://www.un.org/womenwatch/osagi/pdf/factsheet1.pdf

Women in Digital Transformation LLC & DAKA advisory AB. (2022). (rep.). *Gender Digital Divide Index Report 2022.* alexpublishers.ru. Retrieved July 5, 2022, from https://gddindex.com/wp-content/uploads/2022/02/GDDI-Report-2022.pdf

Chapter 7

Gender Disparities in Cryptocurrencies: Perspectives from Developing and Emerging Economies

Sheena Lovia Boateng

University of Ghana Business School, University of Ghana, P O Box LG 78, Legon, Ghana

Contents

Introduction

Fin-tech can be broadly defined as "technologically enabled financial innovation that could result in new business models, applications, processes, or products with an associated material effect on financial markets and institutions and the provision of financial services" (Basel Committee on

Banking Supervision, 2018, p. 8). Major fin-tech products include blockchain technology and cryptocurrencies. Blockchain represents a decentralized database, a ledger, containing information stored in interconnected blocks that create an irreversible timeline of data; after storing, the information cannot be changed (Hayes, 2022). In turn, cryptocurrency is a virtual (digital) currency stored and created on blockchain and protected by encryption (Frankenfield, 2022).

In recent years, the technological revolution, coupled with the accelerated acceptance of digital technology due to the COVID-19 pandemic, has led to a significant change in access to finance (Bollaert et al., 2021; Buchak et al., 2018; Demirgüç-Kunt et al., 2022). To date, 71% of adults in developing economies own a formal financial account, compared to a mere 42% a decade ago (Demirgüç-Kunt et al., 2022). Moreover, the gender gap in access to finance in developing economies has decreased from 9 to 6 percentage points (Demirgüç-Kunt et al., 2022).

The recent COVID-19 pandemic has led to a significant increase in the usage of digital financial services (Demirgüç-Kunt et al., 2022; OECD, 2020). Available evidence suggests that, since the pandemic outbreak, approximately 40% of adults in developing economies (excluding China) made a digital merchant payment, while over one-third of adults in developing economies paid a utility bill directly from their bank account. In Sub-Saharan Africa, mobile money has emerged as a critical driver of financial inclusion, particularly for women (Agur et al., 2020; Demirgüç-Kunt et al., 2022). Mobile money supports account ownership and usage through mobile payments, savings, and borrowing, independent of traditional banking.

Although blockchain technologies such as cryptocurrencies are being recognized as valuable tools that can promote financial inclusion and empower marginalized people, available research on their use among women, particularly female micro-entrepreneurs, remains scarce (Henshaw, 2022; Isaacs et al., 2022).

Overall, there is a broad consensus among scholars that, in developing and emerging economies, the lack of access to technology can be a significant barrier to women's equal participation in the cryptocurrency industry. Another major obstacle to women's participation in the cryptocurrency industry is that women are more likely to be engaged in informal work and less likely to have access to formal financial services. This suggests that, in addition to the general barriers to technology and financial services access, including the lack of appropriate education and role models, there is a further limitation for women in developing and emerging economies regarding cryptocurrency.

In this context, the chapter aims to provide an initial assessment of gender disparities in access to cryptocurrencies, with a particular emphasis on developing and emerging economies. The remainder of the chapter is structured as follows. The next section provides a brief overview of gender disparities in fin-tech in developing and emerging economies. In the third section, barriers to women using blockchain and cryptocurrency, as well as gender disparities in this domain, are discussed. The chapter concludes by discussing the measures needed to improve women's participation in the cryptocurrency industry and fin-tech.

Gender Gaps in Fin-Tech

While, in present-day Africa, the area of fin-tech is still dominated by men, female "techpreneurs" have recently started to gain their place in this field, despite the gender bias that makes it more difficult for women to acquire capital and expand their firms (Bhalla, 2022). Interestingly, Africa has twice as many female-led fin-tech companies as compared to the average on the global level (Bhalla, 2022). However, fin-techs led exclusively by women received less than 5% of total investments allocated to tech businesses in Africa (Bhalla, 2022). This being said, while female techpreneurs struggle with heavier restrictions and lower valuations, the sector has witnessed numerous successful stories (Bhalla, 2022; Nnamani, 2022).

Similarly, in South East Asia (SEA), women aged over 38 years old are anticipated to become a major segment of the fin-tech market by 2050 (Pathe, 2022). Fin-tech offers various financial services to women who own businesses, including loans. Considering that, traditionally, women in SEA have had far lower chances of getting credit approved (World's Women Banking, 2015), fin-tech could enhance women's empowerment in SEA and beyond.

Numerous studies have demonstrated that women exhibit lower levels of financial literacy (Bannier et al., 2019). As of now, women remain to be substantially underrepresented in both finance and technology (Khera et al., 2022). For instance, in a new survey from 28 countries, Chen et al. (2021) found that only 21% of women use fin-tech products and services, as compared to 29% of men. Nevertheless, in this context, fin-tech does show potential for effectively increasing women's financial inclusion, thereby bridging the gender gap in financial service access.

Women's financial inclusion and participation in the financial system are associated with many benefits, such as risk reduction and improving household management in health and education spending (Agur et al., 2020; Kaur & Kaur, 2021). Furthermore, women's access to financial services and ownership of savings accounts can improve the decision-making process and resource allocation. Indeed, as argued by Kaur and Kaur (2021), access to digital services and bank accounts has a beneficial impact on economic development. Accordingly, the involvement of women in the financial system can decrease inequality, boost social well-being, and strengthen a country's economy.

In addition to the positive impact on the economy, there is evidence to suggest that technology and financial advances have greatly expanded the financial system's accessibility and increased financial inclusion (Mittal, 2020). The use of digital innovations has been reported to eliminate geographic and infrastructure barriers for the most vulnerable groups (Bhatia & Mittal, 2019). This makes fin-tech companies essential to increasing financial inclusion and Internet usage, especially among women in Southeast Asia (Sumarsono et al., 2021) and Sub-Saharan Africa (Lyons et al., 2020).

Gender Disparities in Cryptocurrency

How Can Women in Developing and Emerging Economies Benefit from Blockchain and Cryptocurrencies?

Today, the worldwide adoption of blockchain technology is already underway, with several businesses beginning to use it to enhance their operational processes (Beyers, 2022). As of now, this technology has had the most considerable impact on the financial sector in developing economies (Beyers, 2022). People in these economies use cryptocurrencies to protect themselves against hyperinflation and use crypto exchange platforms to speculate (Beyers, 2022). However, the primary barrier to the adoption of blockchain technology in developing countries is volatility (Beyers, 2022). With an increase in institutional interest in blockchain, it is generally expected that the cryptocurrency market will become considerably more stable. And as volatility declines over time, more countries may decide to use digital currencies as a tool to counteract inflation.

Adoption rates of innovative technology will increase as this technology becomes easier to use, particularly in emerging economies where a rise in the use of digital assets is expected to fuel the global economic empowerment of women (Yakubowski, 2021). If provided access to low-cost, high-value revolutionary technology, including smartphone apps, women will acquire a significant potential to close the gender gap. Likewise, women might be empowered by the crypto industry with a broad spectrum of financial inclusion services, from international payments to creating tokens.

The annual Paxful Team's list of the leading female professionals and entrepreneurs in the blockchain and Bitcoin industry in Africa recognizes some of the most influential women in this field (Paxful Team, 2020). The founder of Blockchain African Ladies, who is listed among the top ten influencers on the 2020 list, claims that blockchain enables freedom for women in Africa.

There are many examples of women empowered by fin-tech who continue to support their communities via blockchain and cryptocurrency. For instance, a young woman from Senegal owns a crypto fishery, the first retail business in her country (or even the entire West Africa) that accepts cryptocurrency as a means of payment (Hall, 2022). Similarly, in East Africa, there is a growing number of women leaders in industries related to cryptocurrency and blockchain technology (Atuchukwu, 2023). These women empower other women—primarily through education on the importance of financial independence in the digital era enabled by using cryptocurrencies. However, even in the present-day digital age, there remain controversies over women's roles and perceptions in society (Okoye et al., 2017). Namely, while men continue to be viewed as managers of household finances, women's economic advancement and social standing remain influenced by their husbands' status. These trends harm women's independence and control over finances (Okoye et al., 2017).

One of the outstanding examples against such control is Fereshteh Forough, the founder of Code to Inspire, an Afghan coding school for girls (Warren, 2020). Fereshteh Forough is an excellent example of an inspirational female leader committed to creating a community for girls interested in robotics and coding, helping them earn money using their knowledge. Moreover, she encourages her students to use cryptocurrency to create their own accounts and wallets so their earnings will not be seized by their male relatives. Since the students' family members are unlikely to be knowledgeable about cryptocurrency, they will not be able to control the school students' earnings.

Forms of Gender Disparities in Cryptocurrency

Compared to men, women tend to have less knowledge of the features of Bitcoin (Bannier et al., 2019). Examining the drivers of this gender gap in the United States, Bannier et al. (2019) found that socio-demographic characteristics and personality traits are accountable for a rather small share of the gap. By contrast, about 40% of the gender gap in Bitcoin literacy is explained by actual and perceived financial literacy. And using digital technology does not add to the explanatory power.

Based on these findings, Bannier et al. (2019) concluded that while reducing gender disparities in financial literacy is crucial, another important challenge that has to be addressed is protecting financial security in an increasingly digitalized financial system.

Indeed, the lack of women in the cryptocurrency industry has been argued to be a very 20th-century issue—applied to the financial tool of the 21st century (Cohen & Wronski, 2021). While the financial services sector has long struggled with gender inequality, cryptocurrencies like Bitcoin and Ether have been hailed as tools capable of democratizing the previously closed-off finance market and attracting new and diverse investors. Nevertheless, in a recent survey, Cohen and Wronski (2021) found that men are twice as likely as women to invest in cryptocurrencies. Accordingly, similarly to the trends previously observed in the conventional financial sector, women are also lagging behind men in terms of real cryptocurrency investment (Cohen & Wronski, 2021).

This being said, the most recent data suggest that, on the global level, about 47% of crypto-curious individuals willing to buy a cryptocurrency for the first time are women (Gemini, 2022). Interestingly, while women account for at least 50% of cryptocurrency owners in Israel (51%), Indonesia (51%), and Nigeria (50%), the corresponding proportions of female cryptocurrency owners in advanced nations and regions are considerably lower: 32% in the United States, 33% in Europe, and 23% in Australia.

Furthermore, it has been argued that more women should invest in cryptocurrencies, as having additional funds in their hands can have a significant positive influence on the world's economy (Krishna, 2022). Along with empowering women as they age and assisting them in closing the gender wage gap, acquiring wealth via investments may also benefit businesses and have a positive impact on society at large. Several previous studies documented that socially conscious investors are likely to be young, single women who are less wealthy but are more educated than their less conscientious peers (Krishna, 2022). Through investments, women may achieve their financial goals and bridge the wealth gap. In this context, a portfolio incorporating cryptocurrencies may be a part of the solution.

In terms of major obstacles to buying cryptocurrency, the results of a recent survey revealed that the major obstacle to buying cryptocurrency is the lack of education (Gemini, 2022). Accordingly, on the global level, survey participants were almost twice as likely to think that more educational resources on cryptocurrency would enable individuals to get involved with crypto (40%), as opposed to suggestions from peers (22%). Furthermore, over 50% of respondents from Latin America (51%) and Africa (56%) said they would feel more at ease buying cryptocurrencies if there were more educational resources available. The corresponding proportions of like-minded respondents in the United States and Asia Pacific amounted to 42% and 44%, respectively.

Another major obstacle to buying cryptocurrency mentioned by the respondents is cryptocurrency regulation (Gemini, 2022). According to non-owners, legal ambiguity around cryptocurrencies is perceived in the Asia Pacific (39%), Latin America (37%), and Europe (36%). Additionally, tax complications associated with cryptocurrency ownership have discouraged 30% of respondents in the Middle East, 24% in Asia Pacific, and 23% in Latin America from making cryptocurrency investments.

Indeed, there remain major uncertainties related to cryptocurrencies' global and national adoption and regulation in the future (Feyen et al., 2022). The growth in the use of crypto-assets may have several effects on financial stability, which is currently challenging to assess and monitor.

Given considerable gaps in regulation and weak investor protection (Massad, 2019), monetary authorities will have to create a legal framework that would be both innovative and prudent (Nasdaq, 2022).

In an analysis of the cryptocurrency-related activity in over 130 countries, including the period before and during the COVID-19 pandemic, Feyen et al. (2022) found that, even in countries with high-volume activity, the total volume remained low relative to the GDP. Moreover, retail volume is rather small (less than $10,000), and smaller transactions refer to only 7% of the total volume. To date, the major share of the crypto volume includes Bitcoin, Ether, and stablecoins, with a rather minor but increasing share of Decentralized Finance (DeFi). However, according to the Digital 2022 Global Overview Report, the number of cryptocurrency owners has increased by 37.8% compared to the previous year (Kemp, 2022). Of note, the popularity of cryptocurrencies is higher in developing economies, especially in economies where conventional currencies are more likely to have fluctuations in exchange rates (Kemp, 2022).

Brightening the Future of Women in Cryptocurrency and Blockchain

To fully benefit from fin-tech's impact on gender equality, it is essential to address gender inequalities in general (Loko & Yang, 2022). Among the major factors contributing to the gender gap in the use of digital finance is the fact that women frequently do not have the necessary tools to use digital services, including smartphones and the Internet (Khera et al., 2022). The latest available data suggest that, across low- and middle-income countries, "mobile ownership and use remain unequal" (GSM Association, 2022), and one of the challenges is reaching the 372 million women who still do not own a cell phone (GSM Association, 2022). The impacts of fin-tech on reducing inequality are noticeably smaller in communities without access to the Internet than in those without such access.

Therefore, to fully benefit from fin-tech, it is necessary to close the digital gap via, among other things, investing in technological innovations and expanding the availability of digital infrastructure.

Furthermore, cultural norms in some countries represent a limiting factor to women's financial literacy. In addition, women's global literacy related to digital and technology is still at about 15%. Since the usage of digital financial services has been accelerated due to the COVID-19 pandemic, there is an increasing risk that financial exclusion will continue due to the digital gender gap (Khera et al., 2022). For this reason, policymakers should prioritize investing in digital and financial literacy.

An example of a success story in Nigeria is Ife Durosinmi-Etti, the founder of Herconomy, a startup that supports women (Nnamani, 2022). Durosinmi-Etti accomplished some noteworthy milestones by providing women access to employment, opportunities, and capacity-building workshops. She has, however, always envisioned Herconomy as an accelerator for women's socioeconomic freedom by actively assisting them in increasing their wealth, managing their money, and gaining access to capital for their enterprises. In Nigeria, only a third of women have bank accounts, which prevents them from accessing digital services and diminishes their wealth-generating potential (Nnamani, 2022). Therefore, Herconomy, which now specializes in fin-tech, has taken the first step by releasing a mobile savings software that enables women to save and earn up to 10% yearly interest on their funds. To ensure that women are not left behind, authorities must introduce measures supporting women as stakeholders, inventors, and end users across every stage of fin-tech and Blockchain applications (Evans & Vincent, 2021). To advance the interests of women in post-COVID Africa, researchers also have to increase the evidence foundation related to these novel technologies.

Finally, to address the gender gap in the cryptocurrency industry, it is important to increase women's education and awareness about cryptocurrency and to promote diversity and inclusion in the industry. This can be supported through relevant initiatives, including mentorship programs connecting connect women with experienced professionals in the industry or educational programs teaching women about the technology and its potential uses and benefits. Finally, it is equally important to promote representation and role models of successful women in the industry (e.g., top ten women leaders in the blockchain and Bitcoin industry in Africa) and to address societal and cultural biases.

References

Agur, I., Martinez Peria, S., & Rochon, C. (2020, 1 July). Digital financial services and the pandemic: Opportunities and risks for emerging and developing economies. Research, Special Series on COVID-19, 7, 1–13. Washington, DC: International Monetary Fund.

Atuchukwu, D. (2023). East Africa Women in Crypto: Paving the way for the East African Woman in Crypto. January 14. Retrieved from https://kenyanwallstreet.com/east-africa-women-in-crypto-paving-the-way-for-the-east-african-woman-in-crypto/

Bannier, C., Meyll, T., Röder, F., & Walter, A. (2019). The gender gap in 'Bitcoin literacy'. *Journal of Behavioral and Experimental Finance, 22*, 129–134. https://doi.org/10.1016/j.jbef.2019.02.008

Basel Committee on Banking Supervision. (2018, February). *Sound Practices - Implications of fintech developments for banks and bank supervisors.* Basel, Switzerland: Bank for International Settlements. Retrieved from https://www.bis.org/bcbs/publ/d431.htm

Beyers, J. (2022). Why Developing Nations Are Embracing Blockchain. January 21. Retrieved from https://www.acamstoday.org/why-developing-nations-are-embracing-blockchain/

Bhalla, N. (2022). Move over 'tech bros': Women entrepreneurs join Africa's fintech boom. February 23. Available at: https://www.context.news/socioeconomic-inclusion/women-entrepreneurs-join-africas-fintech-revolution

Bhatia, A., & Mittal, P. (2019). Big data driven healthcare supply chain: Understanding potentials and capabilities. *SSRN Electronic Journal*. https://doi.org/10.2139/ssrn.3464217

Bollaert, H., Lopez-de-Silanes, F., & Schwienbacher, A. (2021). Fintech and access to finance. *Journal of Corporate Finance, 68*. https://doi.org/10.1016/j.jcorpfin.2021.101941

Buchak, G., Matvos, G., Piskorski, T., & Seru, A. (2018). Fintech, regulatory arbitrage, and the rise of shadow banks. *Journal of Financial Economics, 130*(3), 453–483. https://doi.org/10.1016/j.jfineco.2018.03.011

Chen, S., Doerr, S., Frost, J., Gambacorta, L., & Shin, H. S. (2021). The Fintech Gender Gap. CEPR Discussion Paper No. DP16270. Available at: https://ssrn.com/abstract=3886740

Cohen, J., & Wronski, L. (2021). Cryptocurrency investing has a big gender problem. August 30. Available at: https://www.cnbc.com/2021/08/30/cryptocurrency-has-a-big-gender-problem.html

Demirgüç-Kunt, A., Klapper, L., Singer, D., & Ansar, S. (2022). The Global Findex Database 2021: Financial inclusion. In *Digital Payments, and Resilience in the Age of COVID-19*. Washington, DC: World Bank.

Evans, O., & Vincent, O. (2021). Fintech, blockchain, and women in the post-COVID Africa. In Adeola, O. (Eds.), *Gendered Perspectives on Covid-19 Recovery in Africa*. Cham: Palgrave Macmillan. https://doi.org/10.1007/978-3-030-88152-8_13

Feyen, E., Kawashima, Y., & Mittal, R. (2022). Crypto-Assets Activity around the World: Evolution and Macro-Financial Drivers. Retrieved from http://www.worldbank.org/prwp

Frankenfield, J. (2022). Cryptocurrency Explained with Pros and Cons for Investment. September 26. Retrieved from https://www.investopedia.com/terms/c/cryptocurrency.asp

Gemini. (2022). *Global State of Crypto*. Report. New York, USA: Gemini Trust Company LLC. Retrieved from https://www.gemini.com/gemini-2022-state-of-crypto-global.pdf

GSM Association. (2022). *The Mobile Gender Gap*. Report. London, UK: GMSA. Retrieved from https://www.gsma.com/r/wp-content/uploads/2022/06/The-Mobile-Gender-Gap-Report-2022.pdf

Hall, J. (2022). Mama Bitcoin: Fishing for female empowerment with crypto in West Africa East Africa Women in Crypto: Paving the way for The East African Woman in Crypto. March 08. Retrieved from https://cointelegraph.com/news/mama-bitcoin-fishing-for-female-empowerment-with-crypto-in-west-africa

Hayes, A. (2022). Blockchain Facts: What is It, How It Works, and How It Can Be Used. September 27. Retrieved from https://www.investopedia.com/terms/b/blockchain.asp

Henshaw, A. (2022). Women, consider crypto: Gender in the virtual economy of decentralized finance. *Politics & Gender*, 1–25. https://doi.org/10.1017/S1743923X22000253

Isaacs, F., Oosterwyk, G., & Njugana, R. (2022). Leveraging Blockchain Technology for the Empowerment of Women Micro-entrepreneurs. Conference paper (IFIPAICT, Volume 657).

Kaur, B., & Kaur, N. (2021). Bridging the financial inclusion and digitalization gender gap in driving economic and sustainable growth. *Administrative Development: A Journal of HIPA, Shimla*, VIII (SI-1). https://doi.org/10.53338/ADHIPA2021.V08.Si01.09

Kemp, S. (2022). Digital 2022: Global Overview Report. 26 January. Retrieved from https://datareportal.com/reports/digital-2022-global-overview-report?utm_source=Global_Digital_Reports&utm_medium=Article&utm_campaign=Digital_2022

Khera, P., Ogawa, S., Sahay, R., & Vasishth, M. (2022). *The Digital Gender Gap. A Bigger Role for Women in Digital Finance Can Enhance Company Performance and Economic Growth*. Washington, DC: International Monetary Fund.

Krishna, M. (2022). Can Cryptocurrency Help Bridge the Gender Wealth Gap? May 31. Retrieved from https://www.thebalancemoney.com/can-cryptocurrency-help-bridge-the-gender-wealth-gap-5179835

Loko, B., & Yang, Y. (2022). *Fintech, Female Employment, and Gender Inequality*. IMF WP/22/108. Washington, DC: International Monetary Fund.

Lyons, A., Kass-Hanna, J., & Greenlee, A. (2020). Impacts of Financial and Digital Inclusion on Poverty in South Asia and Sub-Saharan Africa (August 28, 2020). Retrieved from SSRN https://ssrn.com/abstract=3684265 or http://dx.doi.org/10.2139/ssrn.3684265

Massad, T. G. (2019). It's Time to Strengthen the Regulation of Crypto-Assets. Retrieved from https://www.brookings.edu

Mittal, P. (2020). Impact of digital capabilities and technology skills on effectiveness of government in public services. International Conference on Data Analytics for Business and Industry: Way Towards a Sustainable Economy, ICDABI 2020, IEEE, pp. 1–5.

Nasdaq. (2022). Cryptocurrency Regulation Summary: 2022 Edition. New York City, NY, USA: NASDAQ Retrieved from https://www.nasdaq.com/campaign/crypto-regulation-summary/

Nnamani, C. (2022). Herconomy expands into a fintech startup with new offerings for African women. October 14. Retrieved from https://techcabal.com/2022/10/14/herconomy-expands-into-a-fintech-startup-with-new-offerings-for-african-women/

OECD. (2020). *Digital Transformation in the Age of COVID-19: Building Resilience and Bridging Divides, Digital Economy Outlook 2020*. Supplement. Paris: OECD. Retrieved from www.oecd.org/digital/digital-economy-outlook-covid.pdf

Okoye, L. U., Olayinka, E., & Nwannenka, J. M. (2017). Financial inclusion as a strategy for enhanced economic growth and development. *Journal of Internet Banking and Commerce*, *22*(1–14), 10.

Pathe, T. (2022). Women Are Rising to the Top of Southeast Asia's Fintech Future. December 3. Retrieved from https://thefintechtimes.com/women-over-38-years-old-to-be-seas-main-fintech-audience-by-2050-finds-robocash/

Paxful Team. (2020). Launches a List of Top 10 African Women to Watch in Blockchain and Bitcoin, in Line with International Women's Month. March 19. Retrieved from https://paxful.com/university/top-african-women-in-blockchain-and-bitcoin/

Sumarsono, Al-Mudimigh, A., & Anshari, M. (2021). Financial Technology and Innovative Financial Inclusion. *Research Anthology on Concepts, Applications, and Challenges of FinTech*, pp. 142–149.

Warren, S. (2020). Diversity and Inclusion in Blockchain and Crypto: The Gender Aspect. Retrieved from https://cointelegraph.com/news/diversity-and-inclusion-in-blockchain-and-crypto-the-gender-aspect

World's Women Banking (2015). Access to Finance of Women-Owned SMEs in Southeast Asia: An Assessment of Five Countries. New York: World's Women Banking. 28 September. Retrieved from https://www.womensworldbanking.org/wp-content/uploads/2015/09/Access-to-Finance-of-Women-Owned-SMEs-in-Southeast-Asia-An-Assessment-of-Five-Countries1.pdf

Yakubowski, M. (2021). Women, decentralization and the world's economic drive: Experts answer. 8 March. Retrieved from https://cointelegraph.com/news/women-decentralization-and-the-world-s-economic-drive-experts-answer

Chapter 8

Digital Access among New Shea Farming Entrants in Ghana

Richard Boateng
University of Ghana, University of Ghana Business School, P O Box LG 78, Legon, Ghana

John Serbe Marfo
School of Business, Kwame Nkrumah University of Science and Technology, P. O. Box Up 1279, KNUST, Kumasi, Ghana

Sheena Lovia Boateng
University of Ghana Business School, University of Ghana, P O Box LG 78, Legon, Ghana

Obed Kwame Adzaku Penu
University of Ghana Business School, University of Ghana, P O Box LG 78, Legon, Ghana

Pasty Asamoah
School of Business, Kwame Nkrumah University of Science and Technology, P. O. Box Up 1279, KNUST, Kumasi, Ghana

Contents

DOI: 10.4324/9781003302346-8

Introduction

The agriculture sector has experienced a technological revolution over the past decade which has the potential to meet farmers' needs accurately and swiftly (Nyarko & Kozári, 2021). This technological revolution includes the development of digital devices and platforms, such as electronic commerce, agricultural apps, and agricultural precision technologies, among others, speeding up communication and information sharing among farmers (Wolfert et al., 2017).

Digital devices have had a significant impact on the agricultural sector, helping to improve the livelihoods of both youth and women (Asenso-Okyere & Mekonnen, 2012). In Ghana, digital platforms such as Agricultural Development Bank's (ADB) e-wallet, allow farmers to access financial services such as loans and insurance. This enables farmers to invest in their farms and businesses, increasing their capacity to produce and sell their products.

While there is recognition of the impacts that digital technologies have on the livelihoods of farmers, those that put a spotlight on the adoption and impact of digital technologies on the livelihoods of the youth and women as new entrants in the agricultural value chain in developing countries remain nascent. We envisage that while technology, specifically digital devices, continue to evolve and become more widely available, it is likely that the benefits and affordances they provide will continue to grow, helping to improve the lives of even more young people and women in the different agricultural sectors, especially in deprived regions of the global south (an example being Ghana). It is in light of this that we seek to examine the adoption and use behavior of digital devices among new entrants in the agricultural value chain, specifically in the shea value chain in northern Ghana. In northern Ghana, shea is a crucial resource for sustaining livelihoods and ensuring food security. The contribution of shea to the income and food security of collectors is reported to be about 21%, and this could be more for some livelihoods (Oduro Akrasi et al., 2021).

The subsequent section presents the methodology used for the study. Then we present and discuss the findings. The final section concludes the study and makes recommendations for future research.

Methodology

This study employed a quantitative approach. Enumerators comprising secondary school teachers, agricultural extension officers, and public servants were recruited to collect the data. Data collection took place from October 16 to 31, 2022. Generally, the response rate was very encouraging. The study was carried out in 217 communities across 28 districts within the five northern regions (Upper East, Upper West, Northern, Savannah, and North East). The selection of the communities was based on their economic status as shea endemic communities. A minimum of ten respondents were randomly selected from the selected communities across the various shea roles. These include pickers and processors, marketers, youth (shea and non-shea engaged), cooperatives and aggregators. For the individual-level quantitative data (i.e., pickers and processors as well as the youth) the response rate was 102.4% which was above the proposed sample size. In addition, for the group-level quantitative data, the response rate was 76.7% for cooperatives and 88.5% for aggregators.

The total data collected at the individual level was 3,077. Over 99.5% of these respondents were females, indicating female dominance in the picking and processing activities in the shea value chain, while less than 1% were males. More than half of males (8, 57.1%) who were engaged in the shea value chain reside in the Northern region. Except for the Upper West region which recorded 100% females, nine out of ten of the respondents in each region were female. This finding of the dominance of women is not surprising since previous research has established that women primarily dominate shea picking and processing, and further, these shea farming activities are culturally known to be reserved for females (Alhassan, 2020; Futukpor, 2022).

Findings and Discussions

New shea farming entrants refer to shea workers who have 5 or less years of practice or experience in shea farming. The findings show that there are 540 new entrants – 30 of them having less than a year of practice and 510 of them having 1–5 years of experience in working in the shea value chain. We focused on the new shea farming entrants because they tend to define the characteristics of future shea workers. On closer examination, there are more females (over 98%), as expected. A majority of the few male new entrants (six out ten) are located in the Northern region. Female new entrants are primarily located in the Upper East (four out of ten) and Northern regions (two out of ten) (Figure 8.1).

The Youth Lead Shea Farming New Entrants

The Youth tend to dominate new shea farming entrants, constituting 68% (about seven out of ten). This is refreshing since as earlier established seven out of ten of the whole shea workers interviewed (3,077) are Adults (five out of ten) and Elderly (two out of ten). On closer examination, three out

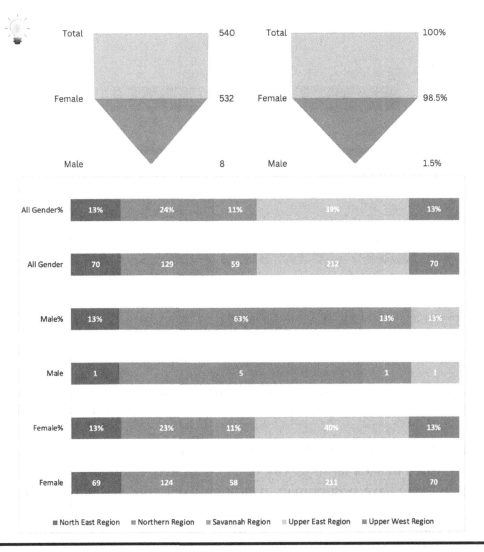

Figure 8.1   Gender representation of shea farming new entrants. (Source: Fieldwork Data.)

of ten new entrants are below 24 years of age, and about four out of ten new entrants are 24–35 years of age. This gives evidence that the Youth are getting interested in shea farming (Figure 8.2).

New Entrants Are Dominated by the Youth and Educated

The findings reveal that there is a slightly larger number of new entrants to shea farming who are educated or have some basic form of education (281–243 Youth, 36 Adults, and 2 Elderly). Thus, about nine out of ten

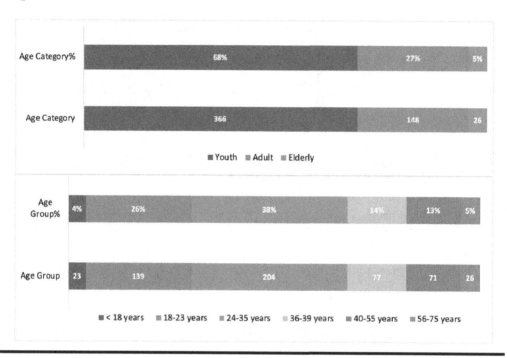

Figure 8.2   Age categories of shea farming new entrants. (Source: Fieldwork Data.)

educated new entrants are Youth, indicating that educated Youth tends to be interested in shea farming. Out of 243 educated Youth new entrants, 134 of them (55%) have post-primary education. Four educated new entrants – two Youth and two Adults – have some form of tertiary education. These findings suggest that the Youth and Adults engaged in shea farming as new entrants are more educated (Figure 8.3).

Pickers and the Married Lead New Shea Farming Entrants

The Pickers tend to dominate new shea farming entrants, constituting 60% (about six out of ten) of new entrants (Figure 8.4). On closer look, about three out of ten new entrants are also Pickers and Processors and about one out of ten new entrants are only Processors. There are also only three new entrants engaged in marketing (two Youth and one Adult). These findings are consistent with the observation made on the general population of shea

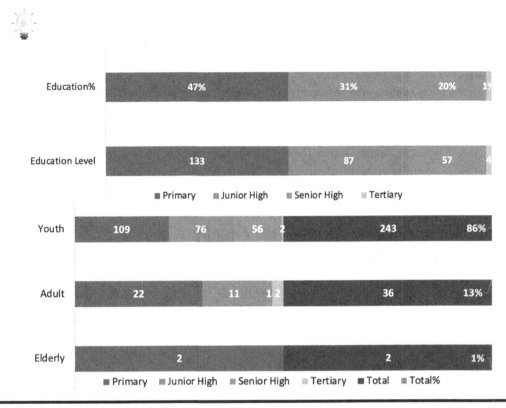

Figure 8.3   Level of education representation of shea farming new entrants. (Source: Fieldwork Data.)

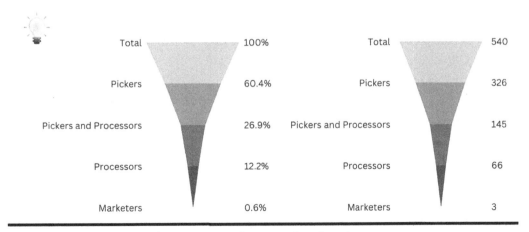

Figure 8.4   Categories of engagement for new shea farming entrants. (Source: Fieldwork Data.)

workers interviewed. Picking tends to be an activity with the least barrier of entry – the least set of skills needed. The complexity of the other activities down the value chain makes it less attractive to new entrants who lack the requisite skills for processing and marketing.

Further, shea farming tends to be communal and, largely, shea workers are introduced into the practice through marriage. In fact, 413 (about eight out of ten) of the new entrants are married. Among the married new entrants, about six out of ten are pickers and three out of ten are pickers and processors. All three new entrants engaged in marketing are also married.

Educated and Non-Educated Are Equally Likely to Join Pickers and Processors

About seven out of ten of the educated new shea farming entrants are pickers and about six out of ten among those who are non-educated are also pickers. On closer examination, there is also not much difference between educated pickers and processors (two out of ten) and non-educated pickers and processors (three out of ten). As earlier established, picking tends to be an activity with the least barrier of entry – the least set of skills needed. Concerning new shea marketers, there is also not much difference since there are only two educated marketers and one non-educated marketer. Per these findings, shea farming seems attractive to both the educated and non-educated (Figure 8.5).

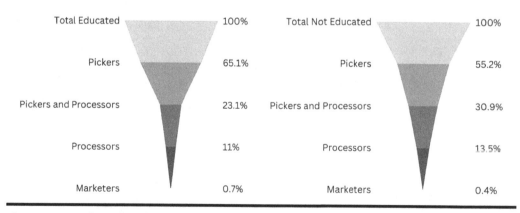

Figure 8.5 Educational level by category or type of new shea farming entrants. (Source: Fieldwork Data.)

New Shea Farming Entrants Earn $30 Monthly

The earnings were categorized into four earnings brackets:

- Low-Income Earners: Up to GHC 500
- Middle-Income Earners: GHC 501–1000
- High-Income Earners: GHC 1001–1500
- High-Income Plus Earners: Above GHC1501

According to the data (Table 8.1), six out of ten new shea farming entrants (62%) earn about $30 monthly. The national daily minimum wage is $1.35 (GHS 13.53). Hence, for a minimum of 20 working days in a month, new shea farming entrants earn an average of $1.5, which is above the national daily minimum wage. The Youth dominate all earnings categories.

Table 8.1   Distribution of Earnings by Category of New Shea Entrant

Earnings Category	Age Bracket	Count	Percentage
High-income plus earner	Total	10	2%
	Adult	1	0%
	Youth	9	2%
High-income earner	Total	16	3%
	Adult	6	1%
	Youth	10	2%
Middle-income earner	Total	73	14%
	Elderly	3	1%
	Adult	17	3%
	Youth	53	10%
Low-income earner	Total	441	82%
	Elderly	23	4%
	Adult	124	23%
	Youth	294	54%
Total		540	100%

Source: Fieldwork Data.

The ten high-income plus earners are primarily located in the Northern (3) and Savannah regions (4). Only two of them have no formal education, and four of them have the highest education level having senior high education (3) in the Northern region and 1 in the Upper East region. These four educated high-income plus earners are Picker and Processor (1), Processor (2), and Marketer (1).

The educated (senior high school) male marketer, located in the Upper East region, is the highest-earning new shea farming entrant, earning $600 monthly and is also a secretary in a cooperative. The second highest-earning new shea farming entrant is an educated (primary education) female picker and processor located in the Upper West region, earning $300 monthly, and is not a member of a cooperative. The third highest-earning new shea farming entrant is an educated (junior high) female picker located in the Savannah region, earning $270 monthly, and is not a member of a cooperative.

The Educated Dominate High-Income Plus Earners but Not High-Income Earners

While eight out of ten high-income plus earners among new shea farming entrants are educated, the situation differs from that of high-income earners. Only about four out of ten high-income earners are educated. The highest-earning high-income earners do not have any formal education, are located in the North East (1), Northern (2), and Upper East (1) regions, and earn $150 monthly. They consist of two pickers and two pickers and processors.

Pickers Are Largely Low-Income Earners

The new picker population are largely low-income earners (eight out of ten). The three high-income plus earners are all female educated Youth (junior high) and are located in the Savannah region, two of them earn $180 and one earns $270 monthly (Figure 8.6).

Pickers and Processors Are Largely Low-Income Earners

On closer examination, the new picker and processor population are largely low-income earners (about eight out of ten). Only 50% of high-income earners in this cohort (two out of four) and 50% of high-income plus earners (two out of four) are educated. The highest-earning new picker

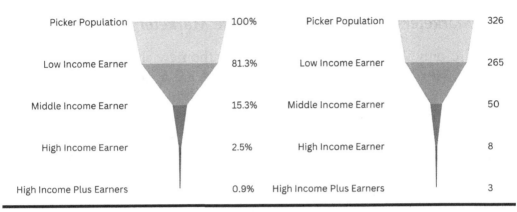

Figure 8.6   Earning levels of new shea pickers. (Source: Fieldwork Data.)

and processor is educated (primary) and located in the Upper West region, earning $300 monthly, and is not a member of a cooperative. The second highest-earning are two new pickers and processors who earn $200, one is educated and the other non-educated.

Processors Are Largely Low-Income Earners

On closer examination, the new processor population are largely low-income earners (about nine out of ten). The two high-income plus earners are all female educated Youth (senior high) and are located in the Northern region, one of them earns $160 and one earns $200 monthly. Two of the four female high-income earners are educated (senior high) and are located in the Northern region, earning $120 and $140. The remaining two female high-income earners do not have any formal education, earning $110 (Savannah region) and $120 (Upper East region) (Figure 8.7).

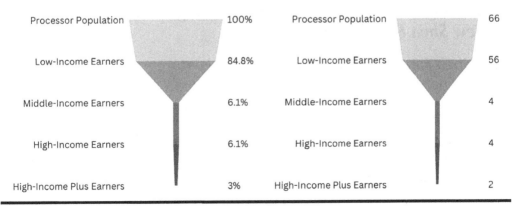

Figure 8.7   Earning levels of new shea processors. (Source: Fieldwork Data.)

Male Marketers Earn Far above Female Marketers

There are only three new marketers among the new shea farming entrants (540). The two female new marketers are located in the Northern and Upper East regions, both earning $300 monthly. The male new marketer is located in the Upper East region and is the highest new shea farming entrant, earning $600 monthly and is a secretary of a cooperative. It presupposes that new male marketers tend to have better access to the market than female marketers, hence, resulting in higher earnings. Comparably, the entire new shea farming entrants consist of two Presidents of cooperatives, one low-income earner ($50, Upper West region, Picker, and Processor) and one middle-income earner ($54, Upper West region, Picker).

Savannah Region Dominates the High-Income Plus Earners among New Shea Farming Entrants

The Upper East and Northern regions tend to dominate earnings categories across regions. The two regions have the highest number of new shea farming entrants in the low-income earner category, and high-income earner category. Further, the Savannah (four out of ten) and Northern (three out of ten) regions dominate the high-income plus earner category. The Upper East (four out of ten) and Savannah (about three out of ten) regions dominate the middle-income category. In short, Savannah region dominates the high-income plus earners and the Upper East dominates the low-income and middle-income earners (Table 8.2).

Influencing Factors for the Adoption of Digital Devices by New Shea Farming Entrants

New Shea Farming Entrants Are Largely Feature Phone-Enabled and Earn More

The findings also show that three shea farming entrants own or have access to desktop computers (Figure 8.8). These entrants consist of two pickers and one picker and processor. The picker and processor and one of the pickers are low-income earners in the North East region and the remaining picker is a middle-income earner in the Savannah region.

Table 8.2 Income-Earning Levels New Shea Farming Entrants by Region

Earnings Category	Region	Count	Total Percentage	Within Category
High-income plus earner	Total	10	1.9%	100.0%
	North East Region	1	0.2%	10.0%
	Upper East Region	1	0.2%	10.0%
	Upper West Region	1	0.2%	10.0%
	Northern Region	3	0.6%	30.0%
	Savannah Region	4	0.7%	40.0%
High-income earner	Total	16	3.0%	100.0%
	Upper West Region	1	0.2%	6.3%
	North East Region	2	0.4%	12.5%
	Savannah Region	3	0.6%	18.8%
	Upper East Region	4	0.7%	25.0%
	Northern Region	6	1.1%	37.5%
Middle-income earner	Total	73	13.5%	100
	Upper West Region	5	0.9%	6.8%
	North East Region	10	1.9%	13.7%
	Northern Region	10	1.9%	13.7%
	Savannah Region	18	3.3%	24.7%
	Upper East Region	30	5.6%	41.1%
Low-income earner	Total	441	81.7%	100.0%
	Savannah Region	34	6.3%	7.7%
	North East Region	57	10.6%	12.9%
	Upper West Region	63	11.7%	14.3%
	Northern Region	110	20.4%	24.9%
	Upper East Region	177	32.8%	40.0%
Total		540	100.0%	100.0%

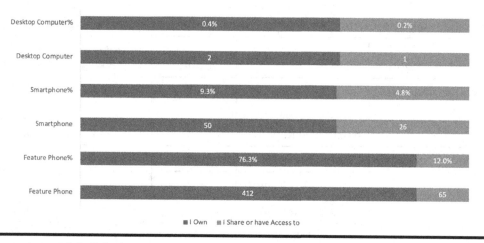

Desktop Computer% | 0.4% | 0.2%
Desktop Computer | 2 | 1
Smartphone% | 9.3% | 4.8%
Smartphone | 50 | 26
Feature Phone% | 76.3% | 12.0%
Feature Phone | 412 | 65

■ I Own   ■ I Share or have Access to

Figure 8.8   Digital device ownership of new shea farming entrants. (Source: Fieldwork Data.)

About 88% of new shea farming entrants own or have access to feature phones, representing 477 (321 Youth, 133 Adults, and 23 Elderly). There are 281 educated new shea farming entrants, 89% of them own or have access to feature phones (Figure 8.9); and 259 non-educated, 88% of them own or have access to feature phones (Figure 8.10). This observation suggests both the educated and non-educated have access to feature phones. Nine out of ten educated shea farming entrants are feature phone-enabled – own

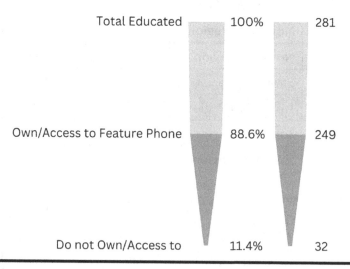

Total Educated   100%   281

Own/Access to Feature Phone   88.6%   249

Do not Own/Access to   11.4%   32

Figure 8.9   Educational level of new shea entrants by ownership of digital devices (own). (Source: Fieldwork Data.)

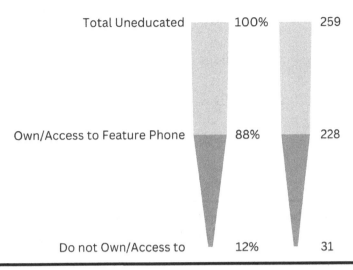

Total Uneducated 100% 259

Own/Access to Feature Phone 88% 228

Do not Own/Access to 12% 31

Figure 8.10 **Educational level of new shea entrants by ownership of digital devices (do not own/have access). (Source: Fieldwork Data.)**

or have access to it (Own – eight out of ten; Access to – one out of ten) (Figure 8.10).

Feature Phone-Enabled Low-Income Earners Earn More than Low-Income Earners Who Are Not Feature-Phone-Enabled

Feature phone users span all the shea farming activity roles – pickers (58.3%), pickers and processors (28.3%), processors (12.8%), and marketers (0.6%). All three marketers among new shea farming entrants are feature phone owners. Further, nine out of the ten high-income plus earners are feature phone owners (8 are educated and one is not educated). Fourteen high-income earners (out of 16) own feature phones, representing about 88%. Sixty-six middle-income earners (out of 73) own (52) or have access (14) to feature phones, representing 90%. Fifty-three of the low-income earners who own or have access to feature phones earn $40–50 monthly. Comparably, only three of the low-income earners who are not feature phone-enabled earn the same. Hence, being feature phone-enabled matters to all shea workers, including low-income earners (Figure 8.11).

Upper East, Northern and Upper West regions lead feature phone ownership and access. The three regions account for eight out of ten feature phone-enabled new shea farming entrants (Figure 8.12).

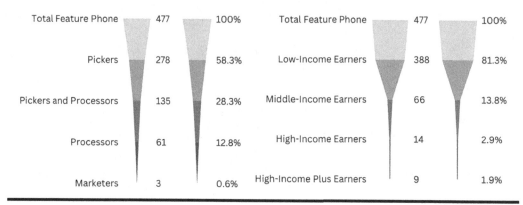

Figure 8.11   Feature phone ownership by category of new shea entrants and level of income earnings. (Source: Fieldwork Data.)

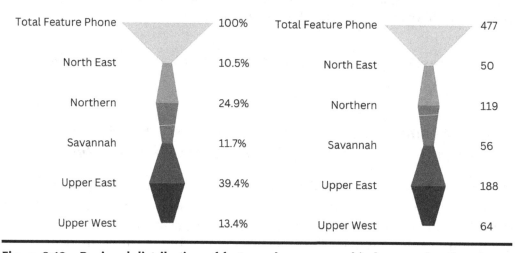

Figure 8.12   Regional distribution of feature phone ownership by new shea farming entrants. (Source: Fieldwork Data.)

Educated Shea Farming Entrants Are Largely Not Smartphone-Enabled

About 14% of new shea farming entrants own or have access to smartphones, representing 76 (69 Youth and 7 Adults). Out of 281 educated new shea farming entrants, only about 21% (59 entrants) of the educated own or have access to smartphones (and only about 11% of the total number of new shea farming entrants) (Figure 8.13).

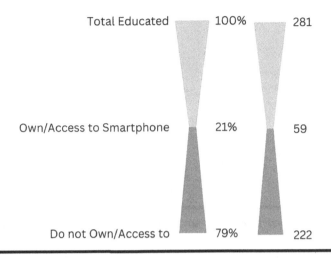

Figure 8.13   Educational level of new shea farming entrants by ownership or access to smartphones. (Source: Fieldwork Data.)

Educated Smartphone-Enabled Shea Farming Entrants Tend to Earn More than Non-Educated Smartphone-Enabled

In actual numbers, smartphone users span all the shea farming activity roles – pickers (53), pickers and processors (12), processors (10), and marketers (1). The marketer, who is the highest-earning new shea farming entrant, is a smartphone and feature phone owner. Further, six out of the ten high-income plus earners are smartphone owners and are educated. However, only 2 high-income earners (out of 16) own (1) or have access (1) to smartphones (Figure 8.14).

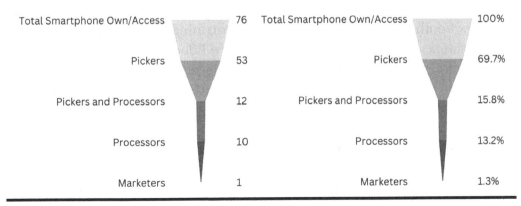

Figure 8.14   Smartphone-enabled new shea farming entrants by activity. (Source: Fieldwork Data.)

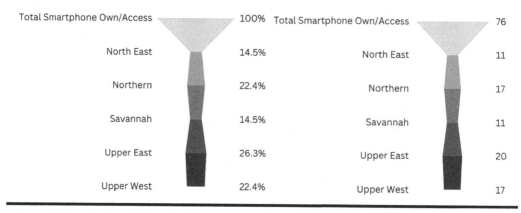

Figure 8.15   Regional distribution of smartphone ownership of new shea farming entrants. (Source: Fieldwork Data.)

Seventeen non-educated shea farming entrants who own or have access to smartphones are low-income (11) and middle-income (6) earners. The few educated shea farming entrants tend to be able to earn more than those who are non-educated. Upper East, Upper West, and Northern regions lead smartphone ownership and access. The three regions account for seven out of ten smartphone-enabled new shea farming entrants (Figure 8.15).

Youth Lead in the Usage of Digital Devices. Adults and the Elderly Do Not Engage in Internet Browsing or Send SMS

All respondents make voice calls – directly and indirectly. From Figure 8.16, SMS messaging and Internet browsing users span all the shea farming activity roles. There are 63 SMS Messaging users. Sixty of the SMS Messaging users are Youth (nine out of ten), and the remaining 3 are Adult (less than 1%). Fifty-nine of the SMS Messaging users are Educated (nine out of ten). All 28 Internet users are Youth. Twenty-six Internet users are Educated (nine out of ten). Twenty-seven Internet users are also SMS Messaging users (nine out of ten). The marketer is a smartphone owner, who engages in SMS messaging and Internet browsing.

As earlier reported, 6 out of the 10 high-income plus earners are smartphone owners and are educated. However, only two of them seem to be engaged in SMS messaging and Internet browsing. Training on smartphone functionalities, Internet usage and how to apply digital devices in shea farming may be needed.

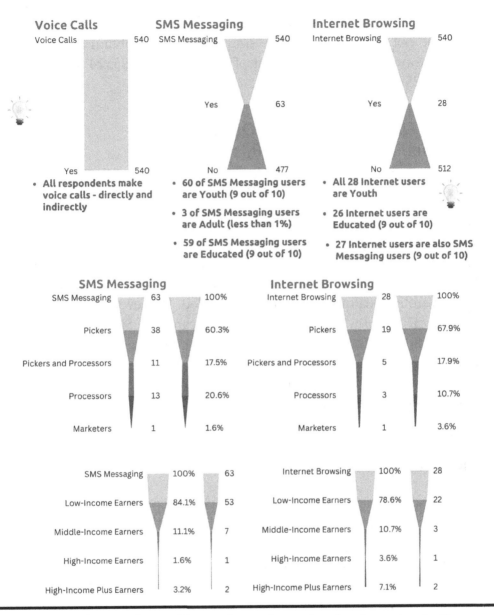

Figure 8.16 **SMS messaging and Internet use of new shea farming entrants. (Source: Fieldwork Data.)**

Need for Digital Use Assistance

Three out of 10 new shea farming entrants obtain assistance from family relations when using digital devices, representing 163 out of 540. Out of the 163, 127 are non-educated (about 78%). Three out of 10 obtain assistance when placing calls, representing 144 out of 540. Out of the

144, 118 are non-educated (82%), 77 are pickers (50%) and 55 are Youth (38%). Nine out of 10 Internet browsing users do not obtain assistance when browsing, representing 25 out of 28. Out of the 25, 24 are educated (96%), and 25 are Youth (100%).

There Is a Difference between Digital Access-Enabled and Digital Functionally Enabled

The data shows that 9 out of 10 shea farming entrants who neither own nor have access to a smartphone report that they can place voice calls on a phone, representing 402 out of 464. Seventy-three percent (293) of these non-smartphone access-enabled do not require assistance in placing a call. Twenty-nine of the 464 can send SMS (27 without assistance and 2 with assistance) and 1 can browse the Internet without assistance. Also, 63 out of 540 (12%) are not feature phone access-enabled. However, all 63 can place voice calls, 37 (59%) without assistance. One can send SMS and browse the Internet without assistance. In effect, some entrants are digitally functionally enabled despite their lack of access or ownership to digital devices, at the time of the study. Affordability could account for the lack of continued access to these digital devices.

Conclusion

This study sought to identify the digital device adoption and use behavior among new entrants in the shea value chain. The findings reveal that the youth are the future of shea farming. The Youth tend to dominate new shea farming entrants, constituting 68% (about seven out of ten). On closer examination, three out of ten new entrants are below 24 years of age and about four out of ten new entrants are 24–35 years of age. Also, there are more females (over 98%), as expected, who are still entering shea farming than men. A majority of the few male new entrants (6 out 10) are located in the Northern region. However, female new entrants are primarily located in the Upper East (four out of ten) and Northern regions (two out of ten).

The educated tend to dominate new shea farming entrants, constituting 52% (about five out of ten). Largely, new shea farming entrants have some form of post-primary education (53%). For the female-educated shea workers, some indicated that they were previous shea workers (family) who left shea farming for school. Thus, they return to the practice after their education or during school breaks or in-between different stages of education. Among the new shea entrants, feature phone-enabled low-income earners earn more than low-income earners who are not Feature-phone-enabled. Forty-three of the low-income earners who own or have access to feature phones earn $40–50 monthly. Comparably, none of the low-income earners who are not feature phone-enabled earn the same, as their income is below $40.

Regarding digital device adoption factors, about 88% of new shea farming entrants own or have access to feature phones. There are 281 educated new shea farming entrants, 89% of them own or have access to feature phones; and 259 non-educated, 88% of them own or have access to feature phones. This observation suggests that both the educated and non-educated have access to feature phones. However, only about 14% of new shea farming entrants own or have access to smartphones (76 entrants). Though a majority of these smartphone-enabled entrants are educated (59 entrants), they are only about 21% of the total number of educated new shea farming entrants. Affordability remains the primary reason for non-adoption.

Practical Recommendations

Digital skills literacy is a primary need for all new shea entrants, who are largely female youth. There is a need to improve access to affordable digital devices for shea workers and cooperatives in a manner that enhances their productivity and ensures access to responsive local technical support centers or trainers to offer training and mentoring in digital skills. Further, for new shea farming entrants training there is an opportunity to offer training in English for the educated, but, training through local languages may be required for the not-educated. Depending on the educational level, training offered could focus on developing the basic skills to identify and use digital devices and navigate the digital world (Internet and social media) and developing the skills to share business information and manage business activities and relationships through digital applications, primarily leading to a sale to a customer or purchase from a buyer. There is a need to train them to operate devices with minimal assistance and also to identify and use specific functions and applications which are beneficial to their shea activities. For the not-educated, basic skills training in writing, reading, and numeracy are needed to enhance their capacity to leverage digital devices and services.

Acknowledgement

We would like to thank the Mastercard Foundation who provided financial support and mentoring for this research as part of a broader study on Digital Needs Assessment for Shea Value Chain in Ghana. Without their contributions, this project would not have been possible.

References

Alhassan, I. (2020). Impact of shea butter processing on household basic needs in selected districts of the Northern region of Ghana. *UDS International Journal of Development*, 7(1), 307–314.

Asenso-Okyere, K., & Mekonnen, D. A. (2012). The importance of ICTs in the provision of information for improving agricultural productivity and rural incomes in Africa. *African Human Development Report. UNDP Sponsored Research Series.*

Futukpor, A. (2022, 11 February). Vice President Launches Shea Landscape Emissions Project, Ghana News Agency. Retrieved from https://gna.org.gh/2022/02/vice-president-launches-shea-landscape-emission-reductions-project/

Nyarko, D. A., & Kozári, J. (2021). Information and communication technologies (ICTs) usage among agricultural extension officers and its impact on extension delivery in Ghana. *Journal of the Saudi Society of Agricultural Sciences*, 20(3), 164–172.

Oduro Akrasi, R., Egyir, I. S., Wayo Seini, A., Awo, M., Okyere, E., & Barnor, K. (2021). Food security in Northern Ghana: Does income from shea based livelihoods matter? *Forests, Trees and Livelihoods*, 30(3), 169–185.

Wolfert, S., Ge, L., Verdouw, C., & Bogaardt, M. J. (2017). Big data in smart farming – A review. *Agricultural Systems*, 153, 69–80.

Index

Page numbers in *italics* refer to figures and those in **bold** refer to tables.

Printed in the United States
by Baker & Taylor Publisher Services